1st edition released November 2014.
2nd edition released September 2018.

To contact Caeayaron Ltd:

E-mail: caeayaron@gmail.com
Home page: www.caeayaron.com
Join Suzanna Maria Emmanuel on facebook & youtube

ISBN 978-1-912214-02-0

Learning To Dance

In Cosmic Love Spaces

To find your inner power

to create change

Ammorah, Pleiadian High Priestess

By Suzanna Maria Emmanuel

Testimonials from Readers

The difference for me between "Learning to Dance in Cosmic Love Spaces" by AMMORAH, and other channeled books by star beings, is the love and light frequencies dancing within its pages.

As soon as I started reading, I could feel the beautiful wisdom of AMMORAH enfold me and the loving Pleiadians surround me.

"This book comes alive with energies of love and light."

I resonated so much with the teachings that I read chapter after chapter until I was gently guided to slow down as I was healing so greatly.

Now each time I read this beautiful book (one chapter at a time!), the loving energies support me in understanding even greater perspectives.

An extra ordinary book. Thank you AMMORAH.

With much love, Glenda Rainey, New Zealand, Star Sacred World Healer, activated by CAEAYARON.

This is more than a book, it is even more than THE BOOK; it is an awakening journey, filled with beautiful star frequencies, healings, teachings, and meditations that help us to unfold as a child of the universe, into greater love, knowledge and understanding of becoming a beautiful flower of love within the universal spaces within.

Throughout AMMORAH shines with great star beauty, supported by the light team of Pleiadian love beings who I often felt around me during the experience of harmonizing and growing into this catalyst of becoming a more beautiful self.

Thank you for the experience AMMORAH and Suzanna Maria Emmanuel.

With love, Stephen Hastings, England, Star Sacred World Healer, activated by CAEAYARON.

A greater more powerful healing book does not yet exist and when one experiences the flows contained within these pages, they will find a strength which is beyond incredible.

AMMORAH will take you on a journey of awakening to your higher star self, your higher love self, in ways that until now have not been possible.

A must read for all who seek the deeper truth for themselves and for humanity.

Thank you AMMORAH and thank you, Suzanna, for this great depth of self-discovery, for the love and for the healing this book has brought me.

With much love and gratitude, Namaste, Jacqui Hanson, New Zealand, Star Sacred World Healer, activated by CAEAYARON.

Wow the magnificence of the frequencies of this book is truly outstanding. Such a great gift of healing, joy and divine love. Every time I pick it up to read it I get excited and feel the love of the star beings around me. I can feel my heart opening and I received many insights on how I can grow greater into the love of my heart.

I can feel myself expanding into higher dimensions of thought as I read the words from AMMORAH.

Every time I get drawn to read it, greater understanding, healing and love comes to me, this is truly a gift from divine, as it is a gift that keeps on giving.

The wisdom in this book is very loving, awakening, evolving, strengthening and beautiful. It is also extremely practical with joyous exercises and meditations for you to work with, to experience greater flows of divine love.

A truly magnificent book to have with you, if you desire to be one with the great star love universes again and desire to help create love and peace on our earth plane.

The wisdom in this book expands our thinking on how we can bring greater love, peace, strength, abundance and joy to our own lives, so that we can work collectively to grow into our greater star families of love once again, to create a whole new consciousness of love on our plane.

A beautiful book to expand upon the awakening journey of HALISARIUS' book Your History Revealed, also channelled by Suzanna Maria Emmanuel.

Thank you AMMORAH and Suzanna for this beautiful gift of love and healing, it truly is a treasure to us all.

Lots of love, appreciation and gratitude, Danielle Roberts, Star Sacred World Healer, activated by CAEAYARON.

What a privilege it is to have this amazing book available to us all, from 'AMMORAH, Pleiadian High Priestess' as channeled through 'Suzanna Maria Emmanuel' the only channel of 'SOVEREIGN LORD EMMANUEL THE GREAT' and 'THE GREAT CAEAYARON.'

As a seeker of 'divine truth' you will gain the greatest of clarity reading the words in this divinely guided book. How to live in 'greater love' is explained in a very beautiful simplistic manner. Written so that each aspect of the information is able to be absorbed fully.

Nothing is rushed or goes too fast in this beautiful book, with the reader able to pick up the information at their own pace. This is not a novel but a 'manual' on how to live a 'greater life' in the 'higher love flows' of 'collective love consciousness.' If your heart desires to understand what is lying deep 'within self' along with what is 'collective love consciousness' and how a person does learn to live in 'collective love consciousness,' then this is a must read for you.

The importance of becoming activated by 'CAEAYARON' through 'Suzanna Maria Emmanuel' and receiving your 'Divine Love Codes' back will be greater understood, when you read and absorb the information presented within the pages. Your 'heart will expand' and your 'desire will increase' to return to a life without the pain, anger, jealousy and envy from the world that currently surrounds you. Each day you will feel more 'peace within self.'

May this book show you, 'who you are' and 'how to reconnect' with yourself and others in the 'higher love flows,' and become part of the 'collective love consciousness' rising upon our earth at this time.

Much gratitude and love, Sharan Collier-Caskey, Star Sacred World Healer, activated by CAEAYARON.

This book is a lifetime resource. As we grow and heal, we can refer back to it and understand each chapter on deeper levels. It is not just any book, but it is a tool filled with healing exercises and meditations. This book helps us with healing different layers, whenever we feel we want to refer back to it, to help us understand the greater love within us and the greater love of the star universes of great love.

Deep love and gratitude to Suzanna.

Much love, Nicole Richardson, Star Sacred World Healer, activated by CAEAYARON.

This book is a pure work of Genius!!! Contained within these pages are great treasures, Spiritual treasures that will help you to understand and 'Dance in Cosmic Spaces of Love'.

Many truths are revealed. So much wisdom is gifted with many exciting exercises. Jam packed with amazing knowledge. Absolutely a must read!!!

With much love, Ngapipi Herewini, Star Sacred World Healer, activated by CAEAYARON.

Dedication

I dedicate this book to the Pleiadians of Light, who care very much about us and our world. I thank them for working so hard with me to be able to bring this information through for the world.

I dedicate this book to the Glorious Universe of Love, to the Great Sacred White Brotherhood, to all Archangels, to all Ascended Masters, to all our Star Brothers and Sisters in the Light, to all Divine Beings on all dimensions of love and light including GAIA, the Spirit of the Earth.

I dedicate this book to our earth who loves us so very much.

I dedicate this book to all truth seekers who desire to understand their greater purpose and understand their precious lives deeper to receive greater meaning and love.

I dedicate this book to all who desire to bring peace and love to our world, to all who truly care and work hard to preserve mankind and our earth.

I thank all in Spirit and Star Beings who have helped me to become the channel that I am, to be able to bring through this important information, for all who desire peace and love in their hearts and in our world.

I thank all my close friends who have supported me on my journey in the light, who have helped me to discover my deeper gifts, who have believed in me and stayed with me all through my time of learning and expansion.

But most of all I dedicate this book to my Divine Universal Teachers, SOVEREIGN LORD EMMANUEL THE GREAT and the

GREAT CAEAYARON, who love mankind so much to allow higher communication and higher consciousness to come through and open the higher gates and portals of Awakening to help mankind return to the light.

Namaste, with many blessings, love and Angel Hugs, from my Awakened Sacred Lemurian Loving Heart, to your Awakened Sacred Lemurian Loving Heart, Suzanna Maria Emmanuel ❤ ❤

Contents

Foreword by Ammorah, Pleiadian High Priestess

A Komo Ha Halima, I AM AMMORAH, PLEIADIAN HIGH PRIESTESS.

I AM here to speak to you about the greatest transition humankind will ever go through, and that is to awaken your energies to allow the higher vibrational waves to come to your spaces.

I speak through the Universal Star Light Grid Programmer, the Divine Love Element of the Great Divine Universe. Her name in this lifetime is Suzanna Maria Emmanuel and she is also known to us by the Pleiadians of love as the Blue star as she is the Archangel of the universes of creation, the Blue Universe of Life on the higher levels.

This book was first transmitted by Suzanna in 2014 when she began to awaken to the higher evolution energies.

At that time, she did not understand her vital role in the universe, and by allowing us to bring these energies to her, it prepared the way for CAEAYARON, MASTER OF MAGNETIC UNIVERSAL FORCES, to work with her as his Universal Light Grid Programmer, and it aligned her to allow her to become part of the Galactic Universal Work ahead.

The healings throughout these pages are designed to prepare you for the Great Activations which began in 2015 upon your earth with the GREAT CAEAYARON, who is the GREAT MOUNTAIN OF LIGHT and his designated Universal Light Grid Programmer, Divine Love Element, Suzanna Maria Emmanuel.

We as Pleiadians of the Great Love are here to guide you to your higher consciousness, to your higher love consciousness, to your higher dimensional growth, to allow you to return to your higher star dimensional states. We consider it a great honor to be part of the great awakening processes and to help you become stronger. We work with Great Divine Will, and we have prepared the way for you to ascend to your higher states.

In this book, I will refer to your Pineal Eye, as the Sacred Eye throughout the book. During the first transmission of the book, Suzanna did not understand the power of the Pineal Eye, the Pineal Gland, and she did not know of the Divine Pineal Gland Activations coming. For her, this book came as a surprise as she did not fully understand that it was all in alignment with Divine Will further on her path.

We are blessing all who desire to become part of the New Rising Love Consciousness upon your earth. We are with you in the Oneness, and those who become activated back to their Lemurian Sacred Light Codes with the GREAT CAEAYARON are considered to be part of our Galactic Family of Light Family. We welcome you back to our Great Love.

During the Divine Activations with the GREAT CAEAYARON, the Galactic Federations of Light witness the activations, and we place special codes within you to allow you to awaken to your higher star gifts at the time when they are needing to wake up.

We work with these same star codes to allow us to truly work as 'One' once the greatest awakening magnetic forces of love come to the universe from the GREAT CAEAYARON, as then we can truly say we are working with one force, with one purpose, with one alignment.

The activated ones who desire to work with the sacred portals to open the higher love flows in the universe upon your earth are working with us, thus they become 'Star Sacred World Healers,' at the Divine Pineal Gland Activations of CAEAYARON. Their Star Bodies open to a higher DNA level and we are privileged to play a sacred part in those sacred levels of awakening the DNA to the higher Star Frequencies, to allow you to return to the greater states of your existence.

I, AMMORAH, PLEIADIAN HIGH PRIESTESS work with you. I work with the Highest Divine Beings of the Greatest Love, and I am on the High Council of the Pleiadian Council to allow our Pleiadian people to be heard. I also hear you and what your needs are. I bring all things to the greater spaces as they need to be heard to allow your prayers to be answered. I am not on my own fulfilling this great task. I, however, as AMMORAH, play a vital task in your awakening frequencies.

I wish you well on your beautiful journey. Discover well our dear friends. Discover the great love and harmony within you. Learn how to grow higher into the love flows and the blessings will come to you.

A Komo Ha Halima, I AM AMMORAH, Pleiadian High Priestess on the Pleiadian High Council.

Introduction by Suzanna Maria Emmanuel

My name is Suzanna Maria Emmanuel. I am a master trance channel, a spiritual medium, spiritual healer, trance healer, a spiritual writer and a spiritual teacher.

Spirit calls me a master trance channel as I am able to hold incredibly high energies of love for long periods of time. I have done this work for many of my lifetimes.

I am the designated channel for SOVEREIGN LORD EMMANUEL THE GREAT. It was He who spoke through Jesus, 2,000 years ago, and now He, the Great Lord, has returned to speak to us again. SOVEREIGN LORD EMMANUEL THE GREAT first began to work with me in this lifetime in 2009.

In 2014, CAEAYARON, known by many as Kryon, approached me and asked me to begin the great work with him also.

I did not know my greater purpose at that time and so I began to understand and remember Lemuria with CAEAYARON. He also gave me back my role as a Light Grid Programmer to help many come back into their Sacred Lemurian Light Codes to help them connect them back into the love dimensions with the Divine Pineal Gland Activations.

I am also a channel for many Archangels, Ascended Masters and Pleiadian Beings of Love.

Pleiadian Beings of Love are here to show us greater ways of living. They are here to help to heal our ways of life so that we can become stronger and greater in our own lives.

They have so much love for us. They are incredibly evolved beings. They teach us about our own higher gifts and help us to remember who we are.

The first Pleiadian book that was transmitted through me in 2014, was by Halisarius, Pleiadian Chief Leader, Chief Commander of the Galactic Federations of Light Societies. He named the book, 'Your History Revealed – How You Are Involved.'

'Your History Revealed,' was about our history and how we can learn to step out of our fear and step into our greatness. Within it, there were great lessons for us with important transmissions, to awaken us from our sleep consciousness to an awakened state of consciousness.

This book from AMMORAH, 'Learning to Dance in Cosmic Love Spaces – To find your inner power to create change,' was also transmitted through me in 2014.

AMMORAH is an evolved Pleiadian Being of Love and teaches us the dance of love and light. She guides us to higher ways of consciousness so that we can align with higher flows to find peace and love in our lives and in our world. She is a wise teacher of light and she is a magnificent light Healer.

Her words of wisdom flow through these pages. Who could have imagined only a few years ago that wisdom like this would flow to our earth to help millions awaken?

She, with all her wisdom, gives us the keys to awaken to our greater gifts of life.

While you are reading these pages, please ask for the guidance of the light Pleiadians to be with you and they will give you deep love within your heart. You will feel them around you. They are always keen to help all who desire to understand the flows of love and light.

I work on deep levels with Pleiadian Beings of Love. When they began to communicate with me several years ago, I saw them and felt their great love pouring into my heart.

They have love that we need to open to, to understand greater love within us.

They have the keys we are looking for, to create a wonderful world of healing and for love.

It is with all my heart of love I give this book to all who are open to the greatness of light.

May you open your heart to love and may you remember who you are. May you see the greatness of the light and open your loving heart to the light. May the Angels rejoice in your joy and in your Awakening and may your days forever more be blessed.

Namaste, always in the great love flows, from my Sacred Loving Lemurian Heart, to your Sacred Loving Lemurian Heart, Suzanna Maria Emmanuel ♥ ♥

About Suzanna Maria Emmanuel

Suzanna Maria Emmanuel is the designated channel for SOVEREIGN LORD EMMANUEL THE GREAT. She is the Ascension channel, designated by Divine Love, to bring millions of people back to the greater love, guided by Divine.

Suzanna is the Universal Light Grid Programmer and Divine Love Element of CAEAYARON (Kryon). CAEAYARON activates people who come to the Divine Pineal Gland Activations, connecting them back into their Sacred Light Lemurian Codes for their great healings and the great ascension. Suzanna works with HALISARIUS and AMMORAH, from the Pleiadian Realms, who are here to guide people towards the Great Love Consciousness.

Suzanna Maria Emmanuel, Divine Love Element, Universal Light Grid Programmer of CAEAYARON and Designated Ascension Channel of SOVEREIGN LORD EMMANUEL THE GREAT.

Spiritual Strengthening
Building the flows of love

Exercise 1: Working with Pleiadians in the light and love

1. Gently breathe in and breathe out. Call your Pleiadian healers in the love to you.

2. You will receive four Pleiadian healers of light around you. Each one is aware of who you are. They celebrate this magnificent moment of being able to heal you and to help you understand your greater self and your greater path.

3. You will receive a Pleiadian Master on your left, on your right, behind you and in front of you.

4. We ask you to relax and to allow a great transmission of great love to be given to you, to allow you to feel our words being spoken through these pages and to allow great healing to take place.

5. When you are ready, allow yourself to come back slowly with the breath.

A Komo Ha Halima

Greetings, I AM AMMORAH

Pleiadian High Priestess on the Pleiadian High Council

Part 1: Introduction by Ammorah, Pleiadian High Priestess

We are here together as your Family of Light and you are also our Family of Light.

My name is AMMORAH, and through these pages I will be introducing you to our Pleiadian realms and also be teaching you advanced ways of learning deeper gifts within you.

I am a great healer of light. I work with many Star Beings and the Angelic Realms. I specialize in opening higher frequencies and higher spaces.

I understand your DNA and I understand how you flow. I am part of a team of great Pleiadian healers who desire to help you understand how to unlock higher patterns within you.

We, as Pleiadian healers, work along with many evolved beings who desire to serve you at this great time. We work in harmony with Divine Will and we understand the great frequencies which will come to your plane soon.

For us, as Evolved Beings of Love, we desire very much to help prepare you for greater gifts to awaken.

Each one of you is beautiful to us. You are like precious songs and you sing sweet melodies in our ears and to our hearts when you desire to sing in the light, as we do.

We, as Pleiadian Beings of Great Love are guiding you with the awakening frequencies. We as Pleiadians, are more evolved than you are. You are an awakening race. You are learning to climb in the higher frequencies of light.

The Archangels are opening up the higher dancing portals for you to play in and for you to recognize.

Through these pages you will discover much about yourselves and how to open up your higher abilities.

You will also understand our ways of the Pleiadians of Light. We play in the Great Light and we look forward to inviting you to play also in the Great Light.

We are inviting you to the Great Cosmic Party of Light. Will you come and join us? You are invited to do so. The blessings will be enormous for you as you begin to flow with your life more.

In this book you will find more about the beauty of who you are and how you are playing in the cosmic dances together with other realms.

These lessons in this book are for everyone who desires to dance higher in life, to understand greater meaning in life, to value light and to define greater light.

It examines how to appreciate the greater self and to have greater abilities to grow higher with telepathic abilities and 'seeing' abilities.

It will give deeper meaning to life and help you to recognize why collective love consciousness is important at this time of your awakening.

It will help you to realize the great love within you and help you to become aware of how important love is.

For those who are ready to take on these higher spiritual processes in this book to create love and peace upon your plane, we welcome you to these higher spiritual processes. You will discover much about expanding your energy centers and create portals of love together.

How blessed you are, our dear friends in the light, to learn these processes. We encourage everyone to read these lessons. Even if you feel you are not ready yet at this time for higher learnings, it will open you to greater flows.

Within these pages, special codes have been placed between the many words you read. These special codes help you in your life, to learn to trust the light, to help you become closer to your Great Self, to help you to understand yourselves in a greater way.

These are healing codes for your greater expansion. Your thoughts will open, your hearts will open, and your lives will become richly blessed.

It is our pleasure to guide you through these processes.

During these grand transmissions as you read these pages, we ask you, for those of you who are willing to participate in this magnificent light, to ask for our assistance.

We keep our promises to you.

May you forever dwell in the love and grow in the Heart Awakening Love.

Your Pleiadians in the Eternal Light, dwelling with Angels of Love forever together with you, dancing the cosmic party of eternal flames of love.

A Komo Ha Halima, Pleiadian Greetings

I greet you with Universal Divine Love.

I greet you with my Sacred Loving Divine Heart.

As I recognize Universal Love within me,

I also recognize it within you,

for we were created with Divine Love Source,

we were created with the Power of the Great Love.

As you recognize the Power of the Great Love within me,

and as I recognize the Power of the Great Love within you,

we stand together in Universal Love,

as Brothers and Sisters,

we stand together as One,

as one Universal Family of Light,

One together,

in the Divine Glory of,

The Great Oneness.

Spiritual Strengthening
Building the flows of love

Exercise 2: Connect to star frequencies

1. Begin by breathing in and out slowly.

2. Ask for the light of the Angels and your Pleiadian healers to surround you.

3. Breathe in their love. During this healing, correct transmissions of light will be given to you to help you connect to the Stars.

4. See yourself sitting on a beautiful chair created with the love of the light.

5. Imagine you are in space, magnificent with light.

6. Visualize stars all around you in this divine place of love.

7. You will connect with one star and ask the star to connect with you.

8. Feel love pouring through you. In return pour love into the star.

9. Slowly come back to your spaces, breathing in and out. Relax.

10. Well done. You have begun your sacred journey, your 'Sacred Dance with the Stars.'

A Komo Ha Halima

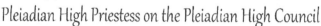

Greetings, I AM AMMORAH

Pleiadian High Priestess on the Pleiadian High Council

Part 2: You have multidimensional bodies of light

Each of you carries tunes from the stars. The stars connect closely with your multidimensional bodies of light to create a space for you to be awakened.

You are in a time when the stars remember your codes and they are connecting with your Higher Light Bodies to create stronger bodies of light to awaken your beauty within you.

You come from the star planets and they are connecting more with you to awaken you to the warped illusion you have created for yourselves, to help you climb out of it, to align you with the stars you are from.

There are myriads upon myriads of dimensions of universes, all carrying life in different degrees which evolve in unique ways to awaken each other to the frequencies of life held within them.

You are living in a time when the stars are calling to you, to awaken to your deeper insights and beliefs.

Star wisdom is filled with ancient wisdom of the universe.

Stars are galactic travelers as they have travelled many universal dimensions, also to gain new understanding to awaken the human race at this time of your existence. They play an important part in your awakening.

You are gifted beyond your belief and knowledge at this moment. You can only step into greater gifts when you learn to step into your Higher Bodies of Light, for then you are learning to program them with higher sequences of the planets.

The stars sing their praises to all who desire to dance with the cosmic energies of love. The star energies are love, and they desire to help you to understand their intelligence. They desire to share their knowledge with you.

Are you ready to experience greater alignment?

Are you ready to investigate the greatest force of the universe within your light body and energy centers?

Greetings, I AM AMMORAH, Pleiadian High Priestess. I am here to guide you home to your love.

You are invited to return to the great love

You have the answers,

within your golden,

loving sacred heart,

your golden secret heart.

You are being invited,

to return to your sacred loving heart,

to return to the light and the great love.

Feel the glory within you rising.

Learn to grow into the love,

of who you truly are,

once again.

A Komo Ha Halima

Greetings, I AM AMMORAH

Pleiadian High Priestess on the Pleiadian High Council

Part 3: Where you can find true answers

Everything is related to each other. All gives life to another. Nothing is disconnected. All is connected to a higher door of learning. All is created with a beautiful frequency. This is a frequency that is clear and is in harmony with higher frequencies.

For many thousands of years mankind has studied the stars. You have always known deep within you that the stars hold many secrets and answers you can greatly benefit from.

What is the relationship with the stars to the secrets within your light body?

Could it be that when you discover your own alignments within your own light bodies that you find many of the answers you have been looking for within the universe?

Your spiritual journey is a journey of looking within, never outside of self. Yet, you send rockets and spend many billions of dollars to search the universe for answers. This funding could be used to feed your people. It could be used to help your people create technology to heal your earth.

Why is it that you spend so much time and money on projects that do not mean your survival?

Learn to care for your people first. Learn to care for your planet first. Learn to tune into your own light bodies. Learn to tune into the wisdom of the stars and the planets to solve issues on your earth.

By learning to tune within your light bodies you would find new technology would come to your plane that could create a beautiful balance upon your earth.

The stars in your system in the universe desire you to listen rather than to probe deeper. You are too immature as a race to go wandering into areas unfamiliar to you.

Learn to solve your own issues first and then the Beings of the Stars will approach you.

A Komo Ha Halima, I AM AMMORAH, Pleiadian Guide and Teacher. We are Pleiadian Light Beings desiring to help you find your light.

Your precious sacred loving heart

Your Sacred Loving Heart,

is precious,

is light,

is glorious,

it is a sacred gift to you.

When will you find it?

When will you be ready to discover it?

When will you see its beauty?

Its love?

Its power?

For all is within you.

Awaken to who you are within.

A Komo Ha Halima

Greetings, I AM AMMORAH

Pleiadian High Priestess on the Pleiadian High Council

Part 4: Dancing with star magic

You have higher subtle energy layers that are awakening to higher tunes. They hear your thoughts and beliefs. They work with flows to shape your beliefs to help you create your 'reality' of your belief patterns you hold within you, to create the magic you believe life to be.

You are your own lawmakers. You are your own creators of your own fields of magic.

How have you been doing? Are you learning to tune into higher waves of magic or are you learning about deeper pain?

The dimensions you are experiencing your life in are saying to you more than ever, it is your choice to experience your 'reality.'

Your DNA is responding to your dance within your belief patterns and is constantly listening if you are open to accept higher codes.

Upon your acceptance your life will take on greater change. However, if you do not accept, you will experience the denser energies greater.

The Cosmic Dance is happening within your multidimensional layers. You become the flows of the dance and the dance becomes the flow of you.

You are able to flow within the body of light and choose to go within. You can also refuse to go within. The choice will always remain yours to have.

Your higher subtle bodies are connected to the star systems and each of your chakra gateways is connected to 12 star systems.

When you open these galaxies within you, you will begin to discover greater galaxies of higher dimensions within you. You will open to higher dances of magic.

You are a small replicate of the Greater Universe. Hence, we say, to find the secrets of the universe you need to look within your being, not outside of your being because you are a small copy, but exact copy, of your Greater Universe.

The greater your understanding is of how beautifully you are made, the greater your acceptance of your higher DNA coding.

You are a ball of conscious energy. You are able to be aligned with higher sun consciousness or the lower pain frequencies of darkness. Those flows are removed from the light consciousness. They instill fear and pain.

The cold lower frequencies are the darker spaces within the universe. These are the parts that do not receive the light of the solar spiritual sun.

The solar sun, or the Great Spiritual Sun, is the key to your awakening to your higher alignment. It has ancient information for you to remember and to learn from.

Spiritual Strengthening
Building the flows of love

Exercise 3: Opening to higher dances of love

1. For a moment, relax and breathe in deeply, then breathe out deeply.

2. We ask you to visualize a great sun with you. Feel the light of the sun coming closer to you. Visualize this sun becoming so light. It shines within your crown chakra and it flows into every part of your being.

3. Ask for the Great Light to be with you.

4. Ask for the love of the Angels to surround you with great peace and love.

5. Ask for a Pleiadian Light Healer to be present with you to help you dance in the higher frequencies of light.

6. We are then placing a rainbow flame of love within you to activate higher dance patterns within your life.

7. We ask you to breathe this in and breathe this out. Be in this light for a few moments.

8. Slowly breathe in and out and allow yourself to come back.

Well done on this sacred dance.

Your sacred power

You are gifted,

with sacred gifts,

from your creators.

They are wise beings,

they can see you,

they know you,

they created your inner power,

they gave you sacred power,

that you have long forgotten.

Now you will learn to find it,

once again,

only when you are ready to learn,

when you are ready to return,

to the sacredness,

within your sacred heart of golden love.

A Komo Ha Halima

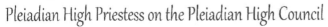

Greetings, I AM AMMORAH

Pleiadian High Priestess on the Pleiadian High Council

Part 5: To find your truth is to seek the dimensions within you

All sacred secrets since times began are within you. Your multidimensional self explains the map of the universe.

To investigate the beauty of all universes is to discover the gateways within you.

Each gateway holds a key to increasing your power. Upon finding a key and then using the power within you, it will open greater gates of inner gifts.

Each one of you is gifted from the stars. The stars tell you to keep looking within. They keep telling you, 'Be guided back to the heart.'

Your heart has sacred codes in place. Your heart understands the foundation of the sacred secrets from the beginning of all of creation and is linked to greater gates of knowledge and of deep wisdom.

Your heart is linked to universal star systems.

You and us together are part of a Galactic System of Existence. We are part of a mighty creation.

Each race in the star universe is made up of unique abilities with deeper gifts given to discover and for greater evolution. Together we are made up of different forces of the Creator Source of All.

You carry the heart of love. We carry the Great Mind for greater knowledge. We also carry the heart. However, your force runs deeper than any other species in the universe because you were created for a very definite purpose.

It is when you discover your heart that your higher abilities switch on.

To understand yourself, your deeper gifts, you must switch on your heart first. Your heart is part of a greater network.

If you can imagine your multidimensional layers as a network of layers and parts that connect to each other via electronic networks, you are on the right path.

When you learn to tune into these layers, you then switch on to create higher evolution.

A Komo Ha Halima, I AM AMMORAH, Pleiadian Guide and Teacher. We are here to teach you how to flow with light to teach you how to find your path back to the Great Light.

Spiritual Strengthening
Building the flows of love

Exercise 4: Discovering inner gateways

1. Begin with the breath in and out.

2. Allow yourself to sit in the light by calling it in.

3. Allow the light to be in your spiritual heart. Breathe in and out and visualize your heart expanding.

4. Visualize a doorway to the Higher Light.

5. Enter the doorway. There are doorways within doorways.

6. Find a switch and see layers of light being turned on.

7. Breathing in and out and let go.

8. Slowly come back and relax.

A Komo Ha Halima

Greetings, I AM AMMORAH

Pleiadian High Priestess on the Pleiadian High Council

Part 6: The heart awakens

You are a force within itself. To learn about the beauty of you, it is important first to understand more about the stars and their higher purpose and then learn about your Creators.

Your Creators created you in the knowledge that your heart was greatly important in the game and the Light Dances. The greater you would find your heart, the greater the portals within you would open, connecting you to your Creators within the star galaxies.

Your Creators have been watching and observing you and are constantly following the patterns of the cosmic planes around you, to see and observe your behavior, waiting to see if you will find your way back to perfection.

You are involved with a galactic experiment to see if you would find your way back home to the Great Light.

The experiment was to find out if you would awaken to deeper discovery within you and to find deeper alignment within your heart.

Your heart is incredibly beautiful with thousands upon thousands of different frequencies running in motion. When each frequency is turned on, it switches to another and then higher frequencies within your universal system are able to plug into these higher frequencies to help you remember your past and who you are.

You are all magnificent beings. It is simply that you have forgotten to play in these energies of light.

Now it is time to understand light more, to define what it is and to learn how to switch on the light within your sacred hearts. Then deeper knowledge and awareness can begin to be understood at this time in your dimensional play.

You are going through many different phases of awakening. Over the last few years, many of you have become more awakened to higher energies. You desire to understand the greater games and the higher dimensional flows within yourself.

'How am I involved?' you question.

We say to you, 'You are involved in greater ways than you realize at this time.'

It is up to you to discover your Greater Self and your greater portals within you, to connect 'home' to the Creators of your existence so they are able to open up greater portals within you to help you discover your greater gifts.

You are incredibly gifted. However, you have forgotten how to keep aligned with the cosmic flows within your multidimensional light bodies. This is why you do not remember how to switch it on, or why you do not remember that it is there at all.

It is as if you have been largely asleep to your Greater Self and you largely have.

Lifetime after lifetime you have experienced life games and desired to have greater understandings. You have learned to search outwards. In your search you have learned to use your mind to question, to use your mind to advance with your evolution.

However, the greatest lessons are made by discovering the beings you are.

You are created from Pure Creator Source. That Creator Source is absolute love. These frequencies of love are pure and great. They are Absolute Love, without beginning or end. It is eternal and you hold these eternal frequencies within you.

You cannot die for true death does not exist. Your higher multidimensional selves exist forever in the dances and the flows of light.

Light is joy and pure love. It does not hold pain that you know of well. In the light you flow with ease and brilliance.

In the greater light, where you return to after your physical death, your higher heart frequencies awaken more. Thus, you begin to explore greater creator experiences. You are able to play higher together as soul families. You are able to create scenery together and flow together in the joy of creating together.

On your plane also, you are creators. You have a great love for creating. You love inventing, drawing, art, music, dancing and writing.

You enjoy these very dances within you as these are part of your creator flows.

Do you understand you are the creators when you invent, draw, dance, play music and write?

You are the ones who are setting the laws and the rules and others simply enjoy and observe.

When you play these laws well, others love your dances of your creation. You are greatly encouraged by them and therefore your heart frequency increases further, and you enjoy dancing higher. You aim for greater because you are feeling the courage within yourself rising. Your strength becomes greater.

It is at this point of discovery, if you play with your love passion within your heart, that your sacred heart connects even deeper with star energies.

A Komo Ha Halima, Greetings, I AM AMMORAH, Pleiadian Light Transmitter and Shiner of Truth and Love.

Remember to play with love

Remember who you are,

remember where you are from,

remember your brilliance,

and you will find your way back home.

Remember to play with stars,

remember to play with love,

remember to play with light,

and you will find your truth,

once again.

Return to the love.

Return to the light.

A Komo Ha Halima

Greetings, I AM AMMORAH

Pleiadian High Priestess on the Pleiadian High Council

Part 7: Connecting deeper with star energies

Star energies are pure creation force. They do not hold onto pain.

Within them is an energy that is alive and thriving, far greater than you realize in your present 'reality.'

When you love doing what you are doing, your light body expands, and it can reach within these star bodies. Some stars will help you with your inventions and you will tap into the wisdom of these stars. Some stars help you with your arts and great architecture. Thus, you are able to tap into the wisdom of these stars. Some stars are helpful and give you higher ideas for creative writing. Your inspiration increases when you tap into these star energies.

You are from the stars. Each star has a different language that your multidimensional selves can interpret and connect to.

On a conscious level you may not understand this. How can you? You have been cut off from the energies of the stars. You cannot remember the greatness of the stars, how they play with your multidimensional selves and how they dance with you at night.

You do not remember and hence you will not remember until you awaken to your star play.

Your multidimensional being is from star energies of love. Love turns it on. It turns it on in higher ways than you realize at this moment in time.

You were programmed by beings of pain and anger to switch it off.

Because you were programmed to switch love off, you never fully discovered true sacred secrets within you.

Your multidimensional selves understand the very essence of your being, which is of love because your Creators created you with the purest source in all of existence, and that is Universal Love.

Hence, love energies will switch you on. Once love has switched you back on, your vibrations begin to increase, your healing powers begin to increase and your energies for your higher creations grow.

You are a magnificent creation, created by your Creators from incredible dimensions of love. Even the ones who desired the darkness could not comprehend the magnificence of your being.

Your Creators are incredibly intelligent. They are far more intelligent than many of the races within the multitudes of streams of beings in the Universal Galactic Existences.

Your Creators knew the great challenge the universe faced and came together to discuss how to birth a species. This species was to grasp the divine knowledge and vastness within a hidden time-lock.

Should the sequences be interfered with, it would shut itself down for a while and be turned on with various light 'sequences' to help you remember your truth within you, when it was time to awaken to your true power.

These abilities that you have are creator abilities. There is no other species in existence that has the power that you are able to connect into, other than your Creators. Within you are creator abilities to move mountains, (literally in your 'reality') and to calm waters.

You refer to the teacher Master Jesus when you talk about the man who could walk on water. However, you can do this also. Has that not been proven in your timeline with people being able to do this?

How do they do it? By being aware you live in an illusion you have created together. By understanding that the illusion can change and by having a strong willpower to prove to the mind that it is different than what others perceive the world to be.

A Komo Ha Halima, I AM AMMORAH, Pleiadian Teacher and High Priestess, dwelling with you in eternal peace, guiding you back home again to the higher star love dimensions, your 'true home.'

Spiritual Strengthening
Building the flows of love

Exercise 5: Connecting to star frequencies

1. Begin by breathing in and out slowly.

2. Ask for the light of the Angels and your Pleiadian healers to surround you.

3. Breathe in their love. During this healing, correct transmissions of light will be given to you to help you connect to the stars.

4. See yourself sitting on a beautiful chair created with the love of the light.

5. Imagine you are in space, magnificent with light.

6. Visualize stars all around you in this divine place.

7. You will connect with one star and ask the star to connect with you.

8. Feel love pouring through you and in return pour love into the star.

9. Slowly come back, breathing in and out and relax.

Open your heart to greatness

Oh human race,

stand in your power,

stand in your might.

Begin to understand,

you are creators,

of your world.

Begin your mighty dance,

together.

Let the light shine down,

upon your plane.

Open your hearts,

to greatness,

within.

Awaken.

A Komo Ha Halima

Greetings, I AM AMMORAH

Pleiadian High Priestess on the Pleiadian High Council

Part 8: You create illusion together

Everyone on your plane carries strong creation forces. Everyone on your plane has thoughts, desires and viewpoints. Everyone on your plane helps to shape and create your world.

Because your energies 'catch on' to what others believe, you see the same things they do. However, although you seem to think that all people see the same as you, everyone perceives everything slightly different.

For example, the way others see a couch, differs with your interpretation of what a couch looks like to you.

You create the illusion together and you are constantly 'reading' other people's energies as to how you think things 'should' appear.

You may wonder about people who live alone. How does this affect them?

But here I ask you, do you not see the power of your creation ability and your energy centers? You create your reality together with your consciousness.

You do not need to be together physically in order to create your 'reality' because you create together with a higher 'wave' of abilities.

If you came together and understood the power you have, you could literally move mountains. You could bring your forests back and you could create water that is clean, all with the power of your collective minds.

You have inherent gifts which are rare in all creation of races in the Universal Existences of Greatness.

It was necessary to create you with these greater gifts because you were involved in the greatest challenge of the universe.

This challenge was raised a long, long time ago. Would you find your way back to light if darkness took light away from earth? Would you respond to Divine Love? Would you be able to transform life back to the way it was, many eons ago?

This is your challenge. We are happy to assist you with this knowledge and deeper discovery.

When you discover it, you will also teach it to us and we will be the ones who will 'catch' on to your powerful energies.

However, these energies are only found when one has found true love within, for these higher abilities cannot be found without true love. These abilities cannot be found without understanding what love is and how to find the greatness for you and for each other.

It is absolutely crucial for you to identify true Universal Love to find these greater gifts your Creators have given you because you were made with their love energy.

The energy they transferred to you is written deep within your DNA centers. These DNA centers run far deeper than you realize. These DNA centers are not only found within the DNA on your physical layers, but also on your higher subtle layers, your energetic layers.

Do you realize, within your higher layers you also have a DNA sequence that energetically sends sequences to your physical DNA constantly? Your physical DNA responds to the higher DNA.

When you understand how you are magnificently created, you will begin to appreciate who you are more.

It is with this appreciation of how great you are that your love energies begin to expand. When these love force energies expand, you begin to awaken the very self within your being because you were created with these love energies.

You are a replica of love. Everything about you is love and you are a force to be reckoned with when you wake up to this. You are a force in itself.

Many people on your plane believe that fear is the strongest force in existence, especially at this painful time on your earth.

At this time, fear is more rampant than ever before in your history. Look at the amount of issues you face as a race together. You are bombarded with challenges, not only in your own lives but also from everywhere else. Your news travels instantly and thus it is easy for you to become overwhelmed with pain.

However, fear is not the greatest and strongest force in existence. Fear itself is a weak energy when it is alongside the power of Great Love. Fear breaks down quickly when the heart truly awakens. Fear cannot stand the Love Frequency and so fear quickly disappears when one truly awakens.

Love frequencies hold the great keys to your greater evolution to move forward.

You will see in the near future that people will decide to go to love because fear will destroy many lives, as it already has.

A Komo Ha Halima, we are your Pleiadian Friends, teaching you how to live in flows of eternal peace and love.

A Komo Ha Halima

Greetings, I AM AMMORAH

Pleiadian High Priestess on the Pleiadian High Council

Part 9: You set the rules for your play

To surrender to love may be difficult for you at this present moment as your expectation of your world is to experience pain, fear and hurt. These experiences have become natural to the race of mankind. However, is it natural to have this much pain?

As an individual you may feel it is because you are used to the hurt. You see much pain happening upon your plane and you may feel it is part of 'humanity' because of the belief you carry.

You may say, 'This is what people do. They hurt each other.'

We ask you, 'Do you truly feel this way?'

Perhaps it is because of your acceptance of pain and how you have given up your faith in the universe and in humanity that you allow pain to happen?

What if you were the creators of all these energies and people who hurt others are playing the role you have given them?

What if they keep playing this role until you give up your play of pain?

Perhaps you will close this book after we have brought up this thought with you. Is this a little much to take for you? Is it too much to ponder upon? Yet, within your heart, if you searched within you, you would agree with our teaching that your world is in the state it is because of your very acceptance that these things happen.

The more you accept your world to be painful, without seeing hope or a brighter future ahead, the more the pain will come streaming in.

When will you begin to see you are the ones who set the rules for the structure of your 'universe?'

Your belief systems within your energy bodies have to play out these stored programs because you are the creators of your 'software.'

You do not understand the power you have collectively. You are constantly creating a different coding for your play to change.

When you feel positive together and inspire each other, fewer tragedies happen in your world. When you are more caring for each other, without shutting each other down, less pain will happen in your life and in your society.

Your earth will also be calmer.

Your energy body affects everything you do in your life. It is your creation machine. It is your manifestation machine.

You are travelling in greater cosmic higher rays. Your time speeds up more every day. You react faster, do things faster, you desire more, and everything is based upon speed.

However, you are discovering you are having less and less time because of these 'time' issues. You are discovering that life is very difficult for you at times because of your very lack of time.

You must understand time is only an illusion created by your minds, created by your energy body, created by your manifestation machine.

You are working in cosmic energies where also your manifestations are working faster. You must learn to make conscious decisions on what you believe, focus upon, and desire as the universe allows you to mirror your belief systems more quickly.

You are walking in a mirror zone. All your thoughts and emotions come into existence for you to act upon.

This is why it is critical for you to understand what you are creating in each and every moment as everything is created constantly and is in tune with the universal rays of the universe.

You are the creators of your world. You decide what you create and how you exist. You have not understood the power you hold within you as yet. You have closed off to the knowledge you had a long, long time ago. You have closed yourselves off from your memory banks.

However, your memory banks are awakening. With it comes the memory of how to awaken to the gifts and the power you hold.

We are helping you awaken because we hold this powerful vision for you. Each day we send out love to your earth and to your people, to help awaken you, to help you to reach out to greater light so that light becomes stronger upon your plane, to help you celebrate light.

Awaken to who you are

Awaken to the light,

awaken to the love,

awaken to your greatness within you.

We hold a vision,

for your hearts to awaken,

to the precious,

golden light.

Reach out to the light,

reach out to the greatness,

awaken to your sacred gifts,

awaken to your inner power,

awaken to your inner strength,

awaken to who you truly are.

A Komo Ha Halima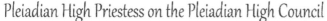

Greetings, I AM AMMORAH

Pleiadian High Priestess on the Pleiadian High Council

Part 10: Your Great Awakening

We work alongside Archangels and many Divine Light Masters of Love with our prayers and manifestations. We work alongside many other Star Brothers and Star Sisters who understand the bigger game. It is you who reached out to light first. You heard our calls and you responded. You reached out to light.

Over the last few years on your planet, your awakenings have sped up. You awaken in waves. You respond to different frequencies.

Some of you have visions and understandings and desire to know the 'unknown,' although many others have been frightened to explore greater depths.

Some of you have been almost in a state of 'passing over' and saw the 'light' before desiring to explore this further to make sense of it.

You desired to journey to a greater depth within you and to understand light and understand your experiences. You desired to understand the greater purpose of your existence.

Some of you have turned to 'light' because of tragedy in your life. You could no longer bear the pain and you desired to figure out how to change your 'reality' of life to experience a higher 'reality.'

Do you not then realize that light is creating a pathway for you to understand your Greater Self and greater purpose?

You are now living in an amazing time of deeper understanding and deeper dances with cosmic energies. You are now being aligned with who you truly are, within your own universal system. This Greater Dance helps you to align you deeper with light.

You are awakening to yourselves.

The awakening within you switches you to a higher frequency. Your cellular memories awaken and you begin to open your mind.

Opening your mind to awakening moments can be frightening for many of you as you do not understand this 'other side' or 'other knowing.'

Your imaginations of the 'other side' may be strong in your mind and because you believe it to be frightening, you may decide not to venture into it.

However, because your cellular memories are awakening, these 'other side' moments may become stronger. Your urges to understand become fervent.

We ask you then, as your star brothers and sisters, are you feeling these urges becoming stronger? Do you desire to understand the 'other side?' Why is it so difficult for you to open to that? Why is it difficult for you to investigate this 'other side' without fear?

This is because many of you have been programmed to understand the 'other side' is something to be frightened about. Many of you have been programmed to believe it is wrong to venture into the 'other side.' Also because of your life experiences, you have learned the trials and tribulations of venturing into areas that do not feel safe. You believe the 'other side' is not safe, as if you will become hurt in one way or another.

We say to you; the awakening is about seeing truth of all of existence. When you awaken and desire greater awakening, your light becomes greater, your understanding becomes deeper, your knowing becomes deeper and your experiences become deeper.

You are in touch with higher energies to awaken your light within you and thus you are feeling closer to Spirit and to your star brothers and sisters.

It is important for you to have an awareness we are here for you, because you know us well, and we know you well.

In the past we played the same dances together and now that you are awakening, we would like to tango together with you once more.

Once again, we ask you then, are you willing to play tango with us? Are you willing to go into a love dance with the awakened ones in the cosmic flows of all existence?

This dance is beautiful, and it is indeed magical for the people who understand the dance and deepen their love within it.

For the ones who desire this, their awakening increases and they become aware of the power they hold over their creation and how everything they focus upon comes into existence.

Therein begins the big transformation within themselves, for they begin to understand that all is an illusion. They begin to create miracles in their lives and learn to bring love into their lives. They learn to bring higher abilities and experiences into their existence. They learn that all flows with light, and the greater the flow is, the greater the experience of love becomes.

They awaken to their creator within.

A Komo Ha Halima, I AM AMMORAH, Pleiadian High Priestess. We are teaching you how to walk with love and dance with greatness.

A Komo Ha Halima

Greetings, I AM AMMORAH

Pleiadian High Priestess on the Pleiadian High Council

Part 11: Learning to dance in your deeper light

Portals of higher gates are opening for you. Those higher gates are waiting for you to discover them. You are able to walk through them to find numerous dimensions to understand your greater purpose in life.

It is up to you to discover them. Each dimension holds a gift. Each dimension holds a secret waiting for you to understand and accept.

These dimensions are within your own Universal Light Existence. They are within your own universal system within your multidimensional beings.

Because you are awakening, you are able to reach within. You may think these dimensions are 'outside' of yourself, but in truth they are within yourself.

You have been looking for these higher dimensions for lifetimes, not understanding how to return to these dimensions to dance these higher experiences of life. You forgot these experiences of these dimensions were within you and now you are learning to dance towards the love dimensions again.

They are waiting for you to discover them. Who do you desire to dance with? Which portal within yourself do you desire to open? Which dimension would you like to have a closer relationship with?

These are all gifts waiting for you to discover. You are a portal within yourself. When you begin to understand the power you hold within this portal of your being, you will begin to desire to master the very portal of love you are.

These secrets have been withheld from you since a long, long time ago. There were many beings who did not desire you to understand these secrets within you.

Why? Because if you knew your true inner power, the dark beings of great resistance would lose the very game they had created.

You are a magnificent creation. You are a creation made with remarkable intelligence, love, existence, power and magnificence. You are afraid to look within because you have an awareness of your greater inner powers. It is only with love you can control your true magnificence. It is only with true love you will be able to find it.

We, as your Family of Light, on our journey of great desire to discover your beauty, asked several questions in order to help you find your way back to your greatness.

Would you uncover the very secrets you hold within? Or would you stay asleep as a race to the beauty of your magnificence? How could we help you uncover your beauty to find the light in your heart once again?

This was a question we raised a long time ago. We desired to understand you more, to help you with your beautiful inner gift of love, to help you discover your incredible truth within.

To answer our own questions, we needed to return to your original purpose. Your original purpose was to bring light back onto your plane, anchoring it within your sacred hearts of love not only to align yourselves back to light, but also to bring back into alignment all existence of life on other star planetary existences.

This was a big task for the Soul Family of Light. After discovering the darkness, how would you discover this precious truth within yourselves once again?

To find the answers, we discussed this in great depth with many members of Family of Light Star Beings, as it was our privilege to help you at this time.

Why? Because you are our brothers and sisters and we desired to help you because you are our Family of Light, as we are also your Family of Light.

To discover the secrets within you we had to go within the frequencies of your hearts, to find your true gateways and to help awaken you when the time was right.

Through all the portals of light, we discovered even more beauty and greater harmony within all existence of all creation.

We discovered life itself and what created life. We became filled with more love for ourselves because it was through discovering you and discovering how to reach and awaken your hearts of love, we discovered our Greater Selves and our greater purpose within us.

We did the journey before you. We came together and awakened our hearts before you. Not only to unify our existences together, not only to find out how to awaken each other here on the Realms of the Pleiades, but also to understand your greater importance.

A Komo Ha Halima, I AM AMMORAH, Pleiadian High Priestess. We are here to help you find your hearts and your Greater Selves.

A Komo Ha Halima
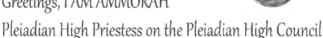
Greetings, I AM AMMORAH

Pleiadian High Priestess on the Pleiadian High Council

Part 12: Our discovery of the core of your existence

We travelled through times of dimensions. We took ourselves back before your existence, before the thought existed to create you, and then we moved forward into the frequencies that created you.

How magnificent it was for us to reach the very core of your existence and to find the spectacular magnificence of you.

To find that light within you, struck us in awe as Star Beings of Light.

You may find this difficult to process. What is it about you that is different to all other planetary races in existence?

We discovered light. We discovered the frequency of love. You would find it difficult to imagine. I will try to help you to visualize what we saw and discovered about you.

We all sat together with the great clear thought and intention of bringing together the frequency of where you first began.

We asked our Creators to guide us with the purpose to help awaken the essence within you and to help awaken the creator within you when it was the time.

We knew if we could access your light, we could guide you in the Awakening Times through the portals and dimensions of cosmic understanding and eternal wisdom.

We travelled back through time. We were taken back through frequencies of time, before the earth existed, before your part of the universe existed, before the stars in your solar system existed.

We were taken to a dimension of Pure Light. This light was similar to a vacuum filled with rays of color, filled with intensive energy, filled with excitement.

This light was pure creation force. This light was enormous and this light was powerful.

Within it was a speck of light. This speck of light was where you were first created. This speck was created with the intention to bring about a species that would carry this light.

This speck of light was implanted within your energy patterns, your DNA patterns and every part of your being. Your cells were created with light. It was pure. It was good. It was perfect.

You were programmed with understanding only love and this love was to be trusted and good.

Before your physical appearance came into existence, you knew that you would create and co create together. You knew before you came here that you were to bring light to a plane that was essentially the greatest plane of all discovery. Its purpose was great.

A Komo Ha Halima

Greetings, I AM AMMORAH

Pleiadian High Priestess on the Pleiadian High Council

Part 13: Deeper explorations within your light body

We were great explorers of your being. We looked at your patterns, at your dimensions, at your frequencies. We discovered much about you and we recorded all we found.

Our scientists made discoveries based upon those findings and thus created probable outcomes. We discussed those probable outcomes before we travelled into your dimensions energetically, to find out if those patterns and our research were correct and we found it was so.

Hence, we could forecast what was to happen when the sacred hearts would be awakened to the Great Light. With this information we could help you discover the creators within you and awaken the love within you to awaken you once again.

You are coming into a time now where your awareness is expanding as greater revelations of deeper purpose is being discovered together by you.

Your questions and desires will become greater as you are opening your hearts and minds to higher frequencies and higher knowledge. As your mind opens, higher revelations will be revealed to you.

These higher revelations hold greater frequencies. They hold vibrational patterns to unlock you to greater levels, to help you understand deeper secrets within you.

Since long, long ago, you have been discoverers of frequencies. You understood the greatest creation force of light and you also discovered the shadows. You discovered love, pain and hardship.

However, all through time, you, the light carriers never gave up on the Great Light returning to your plane.

Through all your incarnations you carried light within, even if you briefly forgot about the Great Light. During your time of forgetting, your discoveries of pain and resentment amplified, and your learnings intensified.

Now, it is the time to dance in the Great Light once again. We invite all those who desire to dance with us, to step into a Greater Dance.

We desire you to step into the Light Dance. The party is becoming greater and whoever comes to the Light Party dances greater with the Great Light.

The Great Light is filled with love and fun. It is enjoyable and it is home for you. The Great Beings who host the party are Love and they desire more than anything to have a closer relationship with you.

Is it within your heart to dance greater and higher? Is it your desire to step away from your pain and fear that keeps your door closed to the Light Party?

Your hosts are your Divine Masters of Love including the Archangels and many other Beings of Great Love. They have created a room for us to gather with you, to help you find your way back to the Greater Light. They help you to discover the greatness of who you are.

Many of you are yearning to find this Greater Party and are asking, 'How can you find the way to the Great Party of Love?'

How will you be invited? Are you invited to the Great Party? You all have an invitation to come and enjoy the party. The food is good. The drink is good. The company is magnificent. However, what will you gain from the Party of Light? Will you listen to the invitation? Why would you attend?

These reasons and gains are personal on your personal Journey of Light. Your understanding of the dance is an individual experience for you. The benefits of attending are immense for you.

You will gain a deeper understanding of who you are. You will understand yourself deeper within your heart. You will understand you are from light and light is part of you. You will begin to understand the very essence of you and that you are part of a creation that is important and crucial to the Game of Life.

Why would you not come? Are you not interested to understand the light within you? For you are personally invited.

Perhaps you have deep beliefs entrenched within you that create a fear to join the Party of Light. Perhaps your anger and pain keeps you away from our party as these frequencies of pain and anger are not part of the Party of Light. Perhaps you are not sure and would like to have a greater understanding of the Party of Light before you join.

These are good reasons why you may choose not to attend the Party of Light at this time on your journey.

You may be afraid of being judged or considered not 'pure' enough.

The hosts of the party are pure love and do not judge anyone. They will lovingly take you by the hand and show you your Journey of Light.

This party is hosted by Eternal Love Beings, who care for all of humanity and for all life existence. Their Power and Eternal Wisdom is beyond your comprehension. They are here to expand your mind, thinking and your being.

We ask you this following question to help you reason within your heart. Are you willing to understand yourselves deeper?

For when you are willing to understand yourselves deeper, you are already playing in the higher dimensions of light and you already sing to a higher tune of greatness.

A Komo Ha, Halima, I AM AMMORAH, Pleiadian High Priestess, inviting you to the greatest love dance journey in the cosmic love experiences.

A Komo Ha Halima

Greetings, I AM AMMORAH

Pleiadian High Priestess on the Pleiadian High Council

Part 14: Your secret sequences within your DNA

When you are in the higher dimensions of play, you begin to open to an inner passion of greatness. You are opening to a higher desire to connect on deeper levels because your heart play is opening to Divine Love.

The Light Dimensions of your creation were pure love vibrations of Divine Love. The play within these energies was Pure Love Force. They were placed within your memories and DNA to help you awaken to higher love frequencies. The play was created in such a way (as you would with a complex computer sequence), to help you awaken to a certain frequency. If you heard this frequency, your passion and greater understanding for greater life awakening would occur.

This gift within you could never be taken away. These were held in secret compartments within your sacred loving heart and your DNA programming.

Your Creators knew the high probability of the DNA being disrupted and interrupted. Hence, they created secret sequences within you to allow you to discover and awaken your creator within you when the time was right.

It was indeed so. Your DNA was interrupted and disturbed. It was taken to bits and split many times, to allow other programming to come within the DNA to allow you to discover fear and anger and thus your true selves remained hidden, until it was time to awaken.

The light within you, dim as it was, stayed alive. You grew into beings who discovered love within you and then you discovered love for the universe. You reached up to the Great Light and the Great Light responded.

You have done well. You are most welcome to come to our Party of Light.

In this Party of Light, we are free to dance the dance we desire. We turn up the music of ancient rhythms to bring us together to a time when we all knew each other well. We dance to the patterns of the ancient rhythms to help remind you who you are and to help remind you who we are.

We dance together. No one dances before the other but each one dances in union with another. We all celebrate each other, and we recognize Divine Union with each other.

We desire to teach you that we do not consider you lower than other races of light in the Universal Existence of creation. We see you as great because we know why you are here and where you are from.

We know you will succeed and we know you will find your way back to the light you are from and you will dance to the greatness in the Party of Light. We consider you as brave fighters for truth and for justice.

You still have some time before you become a Greater Race. You are a new race in the making. You are becoming a New Awakened Race.

We, at the Party of Light, celebrate this knowledge that you are awakening and that you are becoming a New Awakened Race.

We ask you; are you ready to discover new depths within you and learn how to dance higher?

Are you ready to discover your hearts and learn to live from your sacred hearts with love?

Are you willing to search within you deeper?

We as Pleiadians in the light are highly evolved and we have discovered much. We have been your tutors for thousands of years and now we are guiding you back to the Great Light.

A Komo Ha Halima, I AM AMMORAH, Pleiadian High Priestess, helping you to understand how great you are and to discover your sacred hearts of love. I am here to help you discover your secret DNA sequences within you, to help you return to the great love dimensions.

A Komo Ha Halima

Greetings, I AM AMMORAH

Pleiadian High Priestess on the Pleiadian High Council

Part 15: Learning to step into light greater

You are energy and you have energies all around you. You are dancing in illusions of light. These illusions of light play a game with you. They are asking you, are you ready to step beyond the illusion, or are you staying within your limited illusions?

Within the illusion of energy there is much to discover. You discover your life in this illusion, and you discover how much pain you can also have in this illusion. Many of you have discovered pain well.

You can also choose to discover how to walk in higher cosmic flows. These higher cosmic flows bring greater understandings of light and help you discover the higher frequencies of love.

You can play with a variety of energies and illusions. You are always free to choose. It is a game. All of life is a game. You can discover much in your game of life and it is your honor and right to discover your 'reality' of your illusion.

Will you discover the Greater Flows? It is your choice. We ask you; do you have the desire to understand the dance of the cosmic universe to discover your creation powers?

We ask you; are you willing to look at your life differently as if it were a flowing dance, rather than solid and structured?

Your lesson at this time is to discover that there is nothing 'solid' in your life.

Everything flows with movement. You may not see this and understand this at this time.

Your brain is an incredible instrument and was made with definite purpose. Large parts within your brain are asleep. They awaken when your heart of love awakens. When your heart of love awakens, higher abilities are able to be accessed, as higher voltage awakens higher brain activities.

You have an ancient brain and this ancient brain is more important to you than you realize at this time, as much of it has to do with electricity flow and the way it flows within your body.

When you realize the beauty of you, you will understand the greatness within yourselves deeper.

You know much about your physical body. You desire to understand it more. Your passion to understand how you were created runs deep.

Why? It is because you hunger for answers. Where did life come from? Where did it all begin?

Here we go back to your Creators. These Creators were and are still highly intelligent. They have great systems in place for creating new beings.

They begin with a clear and definite purpose. They begin first with Universal Laws. What is the purpose of this particular creation? What is the purpose of higher understanding? How will it work with Divine Will?

They have a list of instructions to follow. These instructions are guidelines. They begin with the basics such as how you will live, how you will explore, how you will find your way back to the Great Light?

Then they build the energy frequencies and these energy frequencies hold patterns within to create the physical layer. All is connected. You cannot live without energy frequencies because you are essentially energy. Your makeup is essentially energy.

Everything within you runs on a voltage; high voltages and low voltages. One may work against the other, which causes disruption and can cause disease.

When you begin to understand this, you will begin to see how important it is to attend the Party of Light.

Your food also runs on a variety of voltages. Your nutrients within your food have a certain frequency that you need for your survival. You may call it different nutrients and it is indeed necessary that you need these nutrients for your health. However, the greater the voltage of the food is, the greater the nutrient content becomes, resulting into greater structure within the human body.

Hence, when you come to our Great Party of Light, you will discover how to increase your voltage of your food to help you stay healthier and younger because you are awakening to knowing how to do this.

Your water is also charged with greater voltage when you understand the 'how's' and you become more greatly energized.

We are trying to point out some great benefits for you to join the 'Greater Party of Light.'

Your memories increase as you join our Party of Light because your brain receives higher voltages and awakens to deeper knowledge and understanding.

Your ability to find deeper discoveries of the human body, grander inventions and grander knowledge increases greatly. Also, your awareness and understanding of your energetic makeup increases, all because you are receiving higher voltages. This is because you are energy and the greater your realization, the more your benefits will become.

When your voltage decreases you become sick. It is better for you to stay happy with an open heart of love than to become sad. Sadness decreases your voltage and your body needs a higher voltage to help you stay healthy.

Greetings, I AM AMMORAH. I wish to send you the greatest love from the Star Beings of Great Love. We are here to help you grow into the love to allow you to return to your higher love dimensions and play in the 'Greater Light.'

A Komo Ha Halima

Greetings, I AM AMMORAH

Pleiadian High Priestess on the Pleiadian High Council

Part 16: Climbing out of the illusion of pain and anger

Returning to one of our previous lessons, you live in dimensional illusions.

It is not until you realize that nothing is as solid as you may believe it to be, that you can begin to party higher in higher frequencies to change your illusion you are in.

Many people on your plane suffer greatly and believe that your life is all about suffering, anger and pain. This is the illusion you are trapped in.

Because you believe it and because it has become your 'reality,' it becomes a greater acceptance among you and thus this illusion increases its strength in your world.

When many people are in pain, you as individuals begin to expect it to happen to you. You begin to believe how bad the world is, and you become more involved with the pain illusion.

Because of the strength of believe in your 'reality' of pain, you forget to open your heart to love and to step into a higher frequency of love. Because your pain is 'real' to you, your pain increases until you begin to understand the 'illusion.'

You are experiencing your creation of pain together because you expect it to happen. If you say you are not expecting it and you are living in pain, how can you say you are not expecting it?

For the ones who are learning to play in Greater Portals of Light, they are able to understand this information because of their discovery of greater ways of playing and dancing.

They are able to understand how to dance higher and create greater experiences together.

For them the game is not how to create sadness together, but instead how to awaken each other to play in light energies and then to observe how their lives become more flowing in the Great Dance of the Great Light.

Can you not see the power of creation within you already? We have only touched the fringes of your own creator power.

A Komo Ha Halima, I AM AMMORAH, Pleiadian High Priest. It is my privilege to work with your awakening flows at this time. We desire to help you understand your greater purpose within you, to allow your greater growth to happen.

Awaken to Creation Power

Holy Universal Light,

allow me to understand,

creation flow,

with all its power,

so that its reality,

can manifest in my life,

so that I may learn to work,

with creation flow,

to awaken,

my creator power,

within me.

A Komo Ha Halima

Greetings, I AM AMMORAH

Pleiadian High Priestess on the Pleiadian High Council

Part 17: The frequencies of thought and power

We will discover the frequency of thought with you. We as Pleiadians also discovered thought-power together. We call it thought-power because thought holds an incredible force. When it is brought together in unity, it creates a greater force within itself.

As you have already learned, everything in the universe is about flow. It is not about being fixed, but about having flow. We ask you to keep this in mind as you journey through these lessons within this book.

The Universe is about flow of existence, flow of life, flow of being and flow of frequency.

Everything in your life flows. When you do not believe it flows, your flows become blocked. Thus, your life will mirror those blocks back to you because those blocks hold within it a denser frequency that 'block' the flowing energies.

Please breathe this lesson in and out slowly and call in the Knowledge of Flowing Existence of all Creation.

To do this, it is relatively simple. You can state, 'Universal Great Light, allow me to grasp the creator flows of all life and of all power, so that its 'reality' can become manifest in my life, so that I may learn to flow with creator flows and with power, to awaken the creator within me.'

When you regularly state this, you will open to higher understanding of frequencies of flow.

The thought is also a process yet to be discovered by you. Every thought holds a frequency within itself. You understand the positive thought and the not so positive thought. You have already discovered this.

Are you ready for deeper discovery and deeper understanding of the energy of the thought?

Keep in mind you were created with the power of thought. Your Creators had a thought together. They used the thought with clear purpose to bring about a creation that would come into existence with many abilities of their Creators. This new creation would discover the higher path to their higher powers of their Creators together.

We hope with this knowledge we are giving, you begin to grasp the importance of the thought. Thought brings into existence life, flow and creation.

Please allow this learning to be absorbed by you for a moment.

If you were created with the power of the thought by Superior Beings of Love and you were created with their abilities, would you not agree you still have much to discover about thought and about how you see your life in your 'reality?'

For many of you, this 'thought' will be incredibly difficult to comprehend because you do not see this Divine Wisdom being reflected into your own lives. Instead, you see pain, anger, bills and disease.

You created your 'reality' together and you also have the ability to create a wonderful, loving space of Divine Union together because of your inherent abilities given to you by your Creators.

Will you be at least open to consider our teachings?

We can give you higher information to open your mind to create greater awareness and help you to begin a life with higher frequencies with greater reflections of flow.

We know your mind likes to understand higher information, but it also likes to keep you in ignorance, repeating the same old patterns to what it has experienced before.

We are trying to help you understand, in order to change your frequencies, it is important to look at your ways of thinking and how you have operated so far in your lives.

Here we are teaching you the flow of thought.

Your thoughts flow continually. They flow in and out and transmit signals constantly. There are higher thoughts and lower thoughts and depending on how they operate, they bring into existence the 'reality' that you believe to be.

Why? Because you are energy and you constantly attract and repel depending on your play of thought and the way you believe your life to be.

If you could open your mind and completely surrender your past thinking and accept your higher voltage thoughts, it would be possible for you to walk into a greater love dimension quickly. For some of you it would be possible to do this instantly.

For many of our readers, this dimensional play is difficult to comprehend. For others it is easier as they have already experienced the process of the greater powers of flow.

The flow of the thought holds a gateway within itself. The thought has dimensions within dimensions of existence. Within the thought there are portals of light and light yet to be discovered.

Within those portals of light, there are deeper dimensions still. When you reach those deeper dimensions, deeper understanding and knowledge will become yours to have. You will find the greater answers and greater power.

This is because the thought holds a vibration that you have not yet discovered.

Each thought is like a portal. Some thought portals are creating constantly, depending on what you are creating and focusing upon in the moment. The stronger your thought-power becomes, the stronger your focus becomes, resulting in a greater energy buildup within the thought portals.

When you understand this, you begin to pay more attention to your thoughts as the flow of your thought is extremely important.

Many of you on your plane have difficulty expressing your deepest thoughts and desires. You do not understand your greater purpose and thus you create greater challenges in your lives with your thoughts. You end up in painful situations with great disharmony and deeper confusion because you are lost and unfocused.

Those who practice higher thought-power, are able to separate themselves from the lower dimensions of thought to step into higher flow energies, to experience a greater understanding of higher love and higher creation.

You are able to create all your desires in a portal of light.

How will you discover this portal of light? You will discover it by joining the Party of Light. The hosts of this party will always guide you to your greatness to discover the love and the creator within you.

You have the ability to live in a greater portal, to create your life in a greater portal, to have greater flow of thought in this higher portal.

When you begin to understand the power within you, you begin to create a magnificent life.

However, your less reflective thoughts and fears stop the flow from your powerful creations and hence your creations become slower to achieve. You give up hope and faith on the way and then begin to drift away from the portals of light.

Your thought-power asks you to tune up your voltage. Do you realize you can sequence your mind to bring more focus and higher 'tuning up' into your mind to help your thought-power to increase?

A Komo Ha Halima, I AM AMMORAH. We are your Tutors, guiding you to higher flows and greater dances.

Spiritual Strengthening
Building the flows of love

Exercise 6: Bring your thoughts up higher

1. We, your Pleiadian Light Healers invite you to do the following exercise. As you do, we will transmit a ray within your mind and energy body of light, to help strengthen your vibration of your thoughts.

2. Invite your Angels and Pleiadian healers to be with you in your present moment.

3. Ask for the Ray of Transformation to your thought patterns to be transmitted to you.

4. Breathe in the light and breathe out slowly.

5. Say the following firmly:

   'I say to my thoughts, run higher. I say to my thoughts, bring in greater power. I say to my thoughts, allow me to run at a greater frequency to increase my thought-power, to use it in the light, to benefit myself and all humanity, to unify myself and the entire universe. I bring myself in alignment with higher thought-power of the universe, to allow higher power of creation to come within me. Amen.'

6. As you say this, you will also receive. Breathe in slowly and breathe out slowly.

A Komo Ha Halima

Greetings, I AM AMMORAH

Pleiadian High Priestess on the Pleiadian High Council

Part 18: Opening your heart frequency to love

We enjoy teaching you and we enjoy joining you in the Cosmic Dances.

We as Pleiadians in the Light enjoy learning higher ways of dancing and we always dance with Cosmic Spaces of Light.

Whenever we come together we celebrate each other and we hug each other because we recognize that everyone, our brothers and sisters, are all part of Cosmic Light.

Together we develop a greater United Cosmic Dance Experience, in love for each other and with each other.

To become greater with thought is to understand how great you are. It is to understand you are important in the Grand Scheme of Dances and Light. It is vital for you to grasp that your life truly counts.

Many people on your earth plane have forgotten the importance of life and lose the greatness and desire to expand.

You have forgotten how to generate greater passion in life and because you carry this reflection of pain within you, it shows in your life because all your 'realities' are a mirror reflecting back to you in your life constantly.

We desire to help you understand that to move forward in life, to learn to dance in the greatness of the Great Light and to play at the Party of Light, it is necessary to understand self-love.

Self-love is one of the greatest teachings in all the Cosmic Party Dances of Light. It is necessary to relate to the light within you and to understand you are from Divine Light. It is necessary to be aware that all exists because of Divine Light, and Divine Light is a part of you.

You must begin to learn to flow with life and higher ways of love and to recognize the Great Love of the Divine One is within you.

Divine Holy Spirit lives within everyone and everything because all is part of the Great One who desired all of us to expand in the Great Light.

It is vital to begin these lessons of self-love. Self-love helps you to see your greatness and your life. Self-love helps you to expand and helps you to realize you are gifted. You have the great gifts of your Creators and you are on your plane for a special purpose. This purpose is to evolve in the light. Everyone on your plane exists to evolve and to help evolve each other.

To be in your awakening lifetime with the awareness, you are going to discover the greatness within you and to feel the depth of your being, which is a great gift for you. It is a gift from your Creators to enjoy.

Be grateful to the universe for these gifts of love. Be grateful to all your extended Family in the Light and to all your Teacher Guides and Archangels and Divine Beings of Love for sharing this vital information with you at this time of the Great Awakening Dance Party.

When you love yourself in this way, when you begin to accept the divinity within you and to see how you are far greater than what you appear to be on the physical layers of your being, you begin to grasp there is a greater internal force within you.

When you discover the greater force within you, greater knowledge will come pouring in because you are ready to comprehend greater cosmic experiences.

Your thought-forms then begin to change because you can see the power of thought creation energy.

A Komo Ha Halima, I AM AMMORAH, Pleiadian High Priestess, helping you to understand the magnificence of your being.

A Komo Ha Halima

Greetings, I AM AMMORAH

Pleiadian High Priestess on the Pleiadian High Council

Part 19: What stops you from creating greatness?

What stops you from creating in the greater dimensions? It is because you do not understand your own significance. When you do not understand self you lose your self-respect.

Self-respect is crucial in the game of light. When you respect yourself, you begin to understand your flows on a profound level of play and you begin to grow to greater depths within you.

When you learn to have great self-respect, your pride returns. Your pride is crucial in this game of play. When your self-esteem is high, you understand the self-importance of your being and thus self-love becomes greater.

This self-love is not ego based. Rather it is love based. All things in the higher dimensions are love based.

People on your plane misunderstand these learnings. Many believe self-love has to do with self-power in a self-centered way.

The way we are endeavoring to teach you is to walk in greater ways of love; to be selfless and not to be selfish. We are guiding you to walk within your hearts and from your hearts in the power of your hearts, in a sacred loving way.

You are afraid to open into the Power of Love. Your fear stops you from using thought-power to create in the higher dimensions of flow and existence.

Your fear uses your thought-power to create in the lower dimensions. Your thought-power controls the frequency of your play in the dimensional game.

When your thought-power creates in the lower dimensions, you attract lower frequency plays to experience the dimension of pain.

When you become angry, you walk in the lower dimensions because these thought forms of anger are lower frequency based, and thus with the power of your thought you are playing in lower dimensions.

We understand it is a trap many of you are playing in and many of you are awakening to this.

When you release yourself from this trap, you will understand its dimensional play of illusions. When you have freed yourself from these lower dimensions, you will face other challenges to release yourself from those dimensions to climb in the higher and greater dimensions.

To play high means to understand higher ways of existence. It means to live with a heart filled with love. To live with a heart filled with love takes dedication and commitment to your journey because you are beginning to see that your life is important. Thus, your self-love gains profound importance in your life.

As you can see, life is a play of illusion.

A Komo Ha Halima

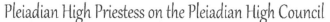

Greetings, I AM AMMORAH

Pleiadian High Priestess on the Pleiadian High Council

Part 20: Unlocking a greater frequency

When you begin to understand thought-power and the importance of your thought, you begin to set rules for yourself to play higher in the cosmic portals of light and dance.

We wonder what your rules will be. Will they include loving each day? Will they include being in peace each day? Will they include meditation to look within each day? Will they include meditating upon your dreams and travelling to Higher Portals of Existence?

Dreams are important to have. Dreams play in Higher Portals of Existence. For those of you who are good at understanding higher plays, you understand the importance of dreaming and being in those dreams. By dreaming and being in dreams, you create a space for your dreams to come into your 'reality.'

You call it visualization. We call it opening a higher dimension and unlocking a greater frequency of play to bring dreams into existence.

Your Creators, as we do also, have the ability to bring their very thoughts into 'reality' instantly. You used to do this too, a long, long time ago. You played with Great Light and were able to bring your wishes into existence instantly. You understood the power of the mind and the way it could instantly manifest.

You used it for greatness and for love. You used the Love Portal of Dimensional Play. You brought in the objective and powered it up with Divine Love of the sacred heart.

This was immense for you. You were clear within your mind and you focused upon what you desired to create. You used the love from your heart to power it up as you would with an engine. This engine of love builds the energy within the Portal of Creation Dimensions.

This in itself is a great lesson for manifestation. Can you see the lesson within this teaching we wonder?

Let us break it down for you.

Thought-power sends out vibrations and frequencies. It creates constantly. Focused thought forms are more greatly powerful than weaker ones. They all come into existence because of the creator force within you.

When you use it intentionally to create your dreams, you focus upon your dreams with your sacred eye. This center is a Portal of Light and a Portal of Creation. This portal opens up higher dimensions. The greater the power of the sacred eye is, the greater the creation is able to be manifested into your existence of play.

Your creations are then powered up by your sacred heart. Your sacred heart is an area filled with love when it is expanded.

To be able to use this for your manifestations, you must work with self-love and self-respect and be at peace. Then, the frequencies within your sacred heart will be perfectly balanced and in the state of sending and receiving.

When the sacred heart is filled with love and you connect to your dreams within the sacred eye center, you are connecting to sacred portals within and you are creating your desires with sacred love.

At first this may be difficult for you. After all, you may have never experienced any teaching like this before and you may feel it is strange to open your heart, or to consider your sacred eye to be this important.

We encourage you to practice, little by little, and then slowly increase it. You are awakening the Love and the creator within your sacred self.

A Komo Ha Halima, I AM AMMORAH. You are being guided to new flows of love and harmony.

A Komo Ha Halima

Greetings, I AM AMMORAH

Pleiadian High Priestess on the Pleiadian High Council

Part 21: How forgiveness plays a part in the Greater Dance

To begin a new life filled with greatness and self-respect is to play the frequencies higher. You will learn how to play within the sacredness of your heart.

We understand the anger many people have on your earth plane. Many people cannot let it go and they feel as if they are locked within their own anger. They feel they cannot play in the Greater Light because their anger has imprisoned them.

Energetically, anger is a prison for you. You are holding yourselves back in this prison. When you release your anger, you are free to move to a Higher Dimensional Play.

You do not understand the power of your anger for anger weakens you.

Learn to be forgiving. Forgiveness is a tremendous force. Forgiveness is powerful, and it is playful.

Forgiveness is about releasing all your painful past and remembering with appreciation the spiritual gifts you received on your journey of love. It is also about appreciating that you are allowing yourself to rise higher in the Dimensional Game of Plays.

The game of anger holds you back. We ask you, what do you achieve with your anger? With anger you close your sacred centers off to your greater expansion. You stop growing with greatness and instead you create denseness within you to create pain for you to experience, until you learn to play the game.

Anger creates illness within you. Anger is a trap and can lead you into many pitfalls.

Can you not see it is better to let go of your anger and to create peace with yourself and with your brothers and sisters? Anger stops your higher growth. Anger stops your progress, individually and as a race. To advance as a race, to come to a greater realization of your internal power, you must learn to be at peace within your heart and with each other first.

Peace is the answer, not war and pain.

When you learn to forgive each other and to forgive yourself, you will come to be in a higher state of being, into a greater state of growth.

You then begin to understand that you were created with great love, for love turns you on and it fills your heart with love and divine understanding.

You are not meant to carry anger. You were not created with anger. You are meant to live in the love, for the love carries a vibration you have not yet discovered at this moment in your time frame.

In the love you begin to dance in the higher 'realities' of existence. In the higher existence of love you create, you manifest, you heal and learn to have peace.

It is love that is your answer to all your issues and challenges in your lives together. It is time you grasped this fundamental truth.

Many people on your plane believe love and having love for others is a weakness, not strength. We say it is the opposite. In love you grow, in love you create, in love you heal and in love you exist.

You come from the Great Light and you heal in the Great Light.

Light is eternal. Light is everywhere you are, and you are living in the light. However, it depends on your thought-power process and self-love to understand this and to reach these higher dimensions. It takes internal self-power to learn to play within the higher spaces of your plays of love.

In the higher spaces of love, you create greater plays of love and you create it well.

We ask you to play there often. As you do, you are ready to play at the Great Party of Light. You will be taught how to play higher and to play it well.

We, as Tutors of Light, always teach with a great respect for all our students. We are not half-hearted beings and we dedicate ourselves to our goals and the way we desire to live in the light.

We are dedicated to guiding you to higher paths, but you are the final decision makers. You are the ones who can make the next move. We can share with you our teachings, our words, our deeper knowledge, our deeper coding within this book. We can give to you our deeper rays of transmissions and healings.

We can speed up your journey to the Great Light, if you desire this to happen. We can share with you our Great Love and our Great Wisdom to help you find your Greater Light. We can give answers you have sought to understand. We can give to you a ticket to the Great Party in the Cosmic Light, but we cannot make the final decision for you.

This, you will have to do for yourselves.

However, for those who are ready to climb higher into your Greater Selves and to your creator within you, we say, 'Come and join us and learn from us, so that we can teach you greatness within you.'

Are you feeling excited? Are you feeling as if you desire to understand more?

A Komo Ha Halima, I AM AMMORAH, Pleiadian High Priestess, holding you in great healing spaces of Divine Universal Family Love.

Spiritual Strengthening
Building the flows of love

Exercise 7: Playing in the light

1. For a few moments, relax and be in the quiet, breathing in and out slowly.   With each breath, allow yourself to become more relaxed.

2. Ask for light to be with you and for your Spirit Guides to be with you at this time.

3. Ask for your Pleiadian healers to be with you also.

4. Imagine you are standing in a field of light.

6. As you imagine it, trust it to be so.

7. We ask you to be playful and to play with light.

8. Which rays of light can you see in the field of light? Which color would you like to play with first?

9. Take a little from the light into your hand and see yourself forming a ball.

10. See the ball growing larger. How big can you make it? Then place the ball in your heart as the light will give you peace and love in your heart.

Well done on your magnificent discovery.

A Komo Ha Halima

Greetings, I AM AMMORAH

Pleiadian High Priestess on the Pleiadian High Council

Part 22: Discovering light to move forward

When we desire to discover and advance as Pleiadian Beings of Love, we always return to the beginning and then we can move forward with greater discovery. This is how we make our greatest leaps forward with our evolution.

Why? Because when you begin at the beginning it takes you into a portal. It is through that portal that greater understanding begins to reveal itself to you.

We never begin from the present, but we always return to the very beginning.

Light is extremely powerful. It is filled with Great Love. Love is the key to all of creation. It is the light and the love together that has an incredibly joyful energy. This energy is a powerful force of the greater dimensions.

Light is a force that cannot be matched. This force is pure creation, pure life, pure knowledge and pure wisdom. It holds within it eternal wisdom, a vortex of deeper understanding.

By returning to the basics of the light we then begin to understand how it generally works.

Its force holds a massive energy that constantly creates power. Its energy field is exceedingly high and anything approaching it would disintegrate. It is Pure Force filled with inconceivable love. We then understand it is a Light Force within itself.

When we reach this conclusion, we then move to the next lesson. We understand when we learn to plug into the force field of light and attach it within our sacred heart, our sacred heart expands in the love and therefore allows the experience of greatness to come into our being.

When we come together as a group and we together hold our sacred hearts in love, we first of all honor each other. We greet each other and we feel the love from each other.

We play in the light together and we sing our higher tunes together. We focus upon the light as we call it in and we plug into the Great Light with our sacred hearts.

Before we do this exercise, we already have it clearly within our minds as to what we desire to bring into existence within our lives.

We focus upon it and thus we are charging up our dream with our very thought-power to bring it into existence, which is fueled by our sacred hearts, thereby allowing itself to be created and to come into our 'reality' of existence.

We work together, completely dedicated to the Great Light with a greater understanding that all is linked together and together we can bring all things into being.

Are we different from you? Of course we are. We are highly evolved Pleiadians in the light. You are awakening to the Great Light.

The gifts you have also come from us, as we have been your tutors in the past and still are at this time.

The time is coming now where you are going to step into this gift together. You will step into your higher mind to create portals of light for greatness to come to your planet.

At this moment, you can as individuals step into these processes.

Please call us in, call in Archangels and all Divine Beings of Love who desire the same as you. We will hold your vision and you will receive many blessings from this work.

How would you like to change your earth? What would you like to bring to your earth that all of humanity could benefit from?

Perhaps you can draw pictures, or paint, or write your stories. When you do this work, your visions already become greater within your mind.

To live with greatness within your heart, you must learn to practice being in your heart every day. Work hard at it, as each day when you work at this, your learnings of love become greater. Greater results will come because this Great Light Work does not go unrewarded.

Love also transforms your mind. Your mind may not always hold thoughts that are of greatness. Its thoughts may tear you apart and take you from one side to another, leaving you in an ocean of unbalance.

However, because love is an energy force with balancing frequencies, it balances the energy frequency of the mind. Hence the mental mind and the emotional mind become more steady and balanced.

You become free to think and talk in greater and higher ways. You will choose not to think in painful ways any longer but instead you will choose to walk in the greatness of your heart, thereby playing in the Higher Cosmic Dances of Love.

A Komo Ha Halima, I AM AMMORAH, Pleiadian High Priestess, guiding you to understand how to walk with greatness in your sacred heart.

Spiritual Strengthening
Building the flows of love

Exercise 8: Open your heart to love

1. Relax by breathing in slowly and breathing out slowly.

2. Ask to be surrounded by Archangels, Divine Beings and Pleiadians of Light who desire to help you feel the love of the Great Light and who desire to have all humanity at peace.

3. Ask for the ray of love to open your heart and to help align you with greater love frequencies.

4. See in your mind one part of earth you would like to see changed. See yourself joining others with the same thought and love.

5. Feel your heart pouring in love to this part and feel how wonderful it is to be a grand part of the change.

6. Afterwards, relax and let go of this sacred space.

7. Thank all the magnificent Light Beings who were present with you, supporting you with their love and wisdom.

8. Slowly breathing in and out until you are fully back.

A Komo Ha Halima

Greetings, I AM AMMORAH

Pleiadian High Priestess on the Pleiadian High Council

Part 23: The awakening of your heart in love

You have a spiritual heart and a physical heart. The physical heart could not live without the Spiritual Dimensional Heart as it receives life-force energy through the gateways to the Great Light. For good health these must be in balance with each other.

Your higher spiritual emotional heart becomes filled with greatness and love and it fills its love within your physical heart.

Your physical heart pumps energy as well as blood. It is a powerful force within your physical layers of your body. It in itself is a force of power.

Your physical heart expands and heals in love. It is affected by emotions and depending on the type of frequency flow of emotion whether it is pain, fear, anger or love it will pump that certain energy flow throughout your body.

Your cells need this vital heart energy. It keeps your cells strong with love and greatness. It breathes in this energy as love holds a high electrical frequency.

When you work with light and allow light to come within you, your heart awakens and pumps out greater voltage rushes throughout your body and your body heals and balances itself.

Your organs communicate with each other and receive this love energy. Hence, when a person lets go of their pain, fear and anger, their energy is higher and they become healthier as a result.

When a person holds fear, pain and deep anger, their organs do not communicate well with painful flow. They are not in alignment with each other and hence disease or great imbalance can occur.

Here we are referring once again to the voltages within your body. Can you relate to yourself as being energy, filled with life and greatness?

This energy force within you is able to be increased or decreased. It is able to create or destruct depending on the voltage of the thought-power.

Thought-power also decreases or increases the voltage and force field range within the heart and thus creates you as a stronger, a more powerful human or a weak, pained human.

The choice, like always, is yours to have.

To find the creator within you, you must learn to work with the energy of your spiritual heart.

You must learn to open your heart force field, so that greater energy flows within you and around you, to allow you to have greater physical health, mental health, emotional health and a greater balanced spirit.

Spiritual Strengthening
Building the flows of love

Exercise 9: Work with the emotional gateway within your spiritual heart

1. This exercise will help you to align your emotional heart with your physical heart for greater healing and love.

2. To do this exercise, please be relaxed to allow yourself to come to deep peace.

3. Ask to be surrounded by light from light beings who care about you. Also call in your Pleiadian healers of light.

4. Trust it is perfect because light beings can see within you and understand how to balance your spiritual emotional heart for greater alignment.

5. With the breath in and out, feel greater peace flowing through you.

6. Imagine for a moment, you are focusing in on your heart, within your deeper emotions. You desire very much to feel more love and to release all sadness, pain and anger to align yourself deeper.

7. Allow yourself to let go of all that has held you back. Allow the Angels around you to take it away.

8. When you have done this, allow their greater love to come in as Angels transmit a healing to you.

9. Breathe this healing in and out. This greater love will give you deeper understanding of the greatness you are.

10. Bring this in deeper and allow your emotions to flow with tears if you feel you are.

11. Breathe in and out deeply and slowly come back.

Well done.

A Komo Ha Halima

Greetings, I AM AMMORAH

Pleiadian High Priestess on the Pleiadian High Council

Part 24: Learn to awaken your spirit within

Your spirit within you creates constantly and desires more than anything to awaken to your love. The greater the love force grows within your sacred heart, the greater the power of your spirit becomes, to awaken you to your inner beauty and inner power.

You are far greater than only your physical self. What keeps your physical body well and alive? Is it only the body? But the body in itself is only a shell. What does the body house? Why are you here? What does the body in itself learn if it is the body alone and the body does not have anything else besides the body?

The body has a magnificent spirit within it. Your spirit allows itself to experience life and experience growth because of your physical body. Without the physical body, you could not experience physical love of your physical existence and experience life on your plane.

Your plane is a learning ground for your spirit. It evolves quickly with deeper connection with your mind on the physical realm.

Your mind is part of the Greater Mind. The Greater Mind is far beyond your comprehension at this time of your existence.

Your spirit which dwells within you in your physical being is only a minute part of who you truly are, but it is enough for you to experience life and love. It is a vehicle for growth and progress. It is the most magnificent way to evolve and learn how to live a greater life filled with higher understanding of higher love.

In each lifetime, you are asked to expand within yourself and within your heart. When you grow and understand this, your spirit within you begins to breathe more life with greater realization until you awaken to the magnificence of who you are.

At that time, your true heart awakens and begins to flow more with love as it dances in the light it comes from. Your spirit expands at that time and it breathes all through all your soul.

At the time of your awakening, when your spirit dances greater and breathes with great love, your lifetime will be greatly blessed.

You will reach great heights and expansions. Your love for all of life will become evident to you and you will come to understand the power of Great Love, and the true connection to the Great Oneness in the Cosmic Flows of Great Existence and Great Light.

When you are unawake, your spirit is held in a very small contained way.

This is why, when you awaken to your greater journey, your spirit within you awakens and it grows until it envelops all your cells and your organs. It is then you understand the deeper path within you and your greater life purpose.

This is part of your evolutionary growth, to understand the spirit within you and how it desires to evolve.

How do you communicate with your spirit? By listening to it and by understanding you can talk to it and also realize it can communicate with you.

It loves nothing else more than to communicate with you, as when you learn to communicate with your spirit you grow phenomenally. You are opening yourself to the greatness of all of existence of Great Universal Love.

Your spirit is a teacher for you. It allows you to learn and become great. It also allows you to stay in your small self if that is your belief. Your beliefs within you, are your 'reality' of your mirror which will reflect back to you constantly.

It is when you awaken to your inner spirit that you gain closer communication with your Greater Mind in Higher Realms of Existence. You then open to the greater purpose for you.

You all have a greater purpose and great life lessons. You have individual path lessons and so your experience is different and unique to others around you. You may not see it that way. You may assume everyone has similar ways of seeing the world to you. However, because your 'reality' is based upon your personal belief systems, others have different ideas about how they see life than you do.

You see your world differently because you are dancing your life uniquely to all others and others are dancing their lives differently to you.

We, as Pleiadians in the Light, along with many of our Star Family of Light, dance in higher cosmic waves than you and our dance within our lives is much higher than you are at this present moment.

Because we dance higher at this time than you, we are able to create a higher tango dance for you to dance in as we create the spaces of love for you to grow in.

The greater your spirit awakens, the deeper the dance becomes as you learn to dance the cosmic waves of energy flows with your spirit and you begin to deepen within the Sacred Love Flow of Life.

Again, everything is about flow and now you are learning to flow in harmony with your inner spirit.

A Komo Ha Halima, we are your Family in Light, as you are our Family in Light, I AM AMMORAH, Pleiadian High Priestess.

You were created to a song of great love

It is with magnificence,

you were created,

to a song,

to a dance,

of Great Love.

When you learn to flow,

with the pureness of your heart,

your love for your life,

will flourish, prosper and grow.

A Komo Ha Halima

Greetings, I AM AMMORAH

Pleiadian High Priestess on the Pleiadian High Council

Part 25: The dance of your spirit within you

Your spirit has a consciousness of its own. It dwells in love and thus when you awaken to the Great Love Force within you, your spirit becomes greater within you.

Your spirit is playful in the Dance of Light and the greater you consciously play in the Dance of Light, the greater the play of the spirit grows within you.

Your spirit is happy and joyful. Thus, when it becomes greater with Play of Light when you awaken, you feel happier and your energy increases as your spirit is filled with high energy.

However, to create a greater house or a temple for your spirit to dance in, you must have the right environment and it must be inviting for your spirit to dwell in.

Your spirit will give you great joy and power to create. The greater the flow of your spirit is within your temple of love, the greater your flow of joy and the power to create a bountiful life.

Imagine, always dancing with your spirit in the light. Imagine the joy you would have to discover your spirit of love.

Your spirit dwells eternally with you. It never leaves you. You have always had it. You will never be without it. You will never be left alone.

When you learn to play in the Dances of Light, your gateway opens to greatness and flow.

You will find deeper connection, you will find deeper flow, you will find greatness within you and together you will grow.

Your spirit desires to help you. Your spirit within you is strong. You will find it will strengthen your life and forever you will flourish.

It comes with you on your journeys of life, wherever that space of growth may be. You may dwell in the different spaces of life, but your spirit will always be there.

When you dance with the spirit of joy, when you dance with the spirit of life, when you dance eternally with all of love, you understand the Dance of Life.

The Dance of Life is eternal. The Dance of Life never stops. The Dance of Life keeps growing. The Dance of Life is filled with Great Love.

When you understand the joy of life, when you understand greatness, your spirit within you will become very powerful and very great.

Then you begin to understand your deeper spiritual self as it will show you dimensions of life and it will show you dimensions of truth.

Your spirit within you is a friend, a friend of truth that dwells in the light that lives eternally, a friend of eternal wisdom and a friend of eternal fire, always working with you to create your desires. It never lies to you. It is truth and always will be waiting. It is always waiting for you to Awaken to the Great Light.

When the light within you awakens, it will dwell with you in closer union. It will send streams of energy to you. You will find great joy in your life.

Your spirit dwells within you, eternally, forever in the light. It will give you answers you have been seeking. It will show you the great ways of the Great Light.

This is the dance of the spirit within you. It is beautiful and it is light. It is perfect in every way. For the one who finds their light within, it is a journey filled with magic.

Everyone who turns up at the Cosmic Party of Light will find this joy in their lives. They will find the way to the Greater Dance of Spirit within.

You can find this greater way also when you begin to open to higher flows of greatness and allow it to grow. At first the growth is young and then it will mature with greater blessings and strength.

Grow with yearnings to understand higher flows. Grow with yearnings to find your truth. Grow with yearnings to find greater dimensions within.

For when you search for this growth, your spirit will answer you. You will find the voice within becoming stronger and the urges for greater growth will become stronger also.

You will then choose to look deeper within you to understand higher dimensions of Great Light. You will find the greatness within you. You will find the doors to the gateways of Great Light.

You will find it has always been there, patiently waiting for you to discover.

When you find the Greater Gateways of Light within, you will have great joy, great peace and great satisfaction.

It is in the Greater Gateways you will find inner fire and inner power. You will then build the greater power of eternal flows of love and light.

You will find the great force within you. This is the force that created you, the force that allowed you to experience the physical play of light.

You are living in dimensions of light and discovering higher growth. You are discovering how to play in the greatness of love. You are discovering the greatness of play and seeking to find your creator within.

When you find your creator within, your play of life deepens more and your yearnings for love become stronger, for it is then you understand the greater dimensions.

It is then you awaken to greater play. You awaken to the knowledge that love is a force within you.

When you grow in the force of Great Love, your energy field expands and your potential becomes much greater and your love for life grows.

A Komo Ha Halima, I AM AMMORAH, Pleiadian High Priestess, guiding you to greater depths of healing.

Spiritual Strengthening
Building the flows of love

Exercise 10: Awaken the spirit within you

1.   Begin by breathing in and out.

2.   Surround yourself with Angels and also call in your Pleiadian healers of light. We will hold the space for your perfect growth at this time.

3.   Imagine you are sitting quietly among the great trees in a beautiful spot in your world.

4.   It is quiet, serene and peaceful. You hear the birds and they sing to you with great love.

5.   The great trees carry great wisdom. They know why you are here and they understand how to open greater gateways for you.

6.   Breathe in and out slowly.

7.   Call your Greater Spirit towards you with the clear purpose you are ready to awaken greater.

8.   Invite more of your spirit to dwell within you.

9.   Breathe your spirit into your crown and feel it coming down into your heart.

10. Feel the union between you and your Greater Spirit and feel the Love growing.

11. Slowly breathe in and out and relax. Slowly let go.

12. Thank all Beings of Great Love who supported you with your
    healing work.

Well done on this journey of light. Always remember how well
loved you are. We know who you are, and we desire to support you
to grow into the greater love.

A Komo Ha Halima

Greetings, I AM AMMORAH

Pleiadian High Priestess on the Pleiadian High Council

Part 26: Going within the depths of your heart

To dance with the light that you are and that you have always been, you must be willing to go within and discover the depths within your being.

Many people on the earth plane shy away from going within. They are afraid to find their deeper feelings, to find their deeper senses and to discover that life is not giving them what they truly desire.

There are many people on your plane who resist seeing their own pain, and because of the severe pain they hold within their hearts they seek to control others because of their great fear of losing what is precious to them.

There are many people on your plane who create a supportive environment to support their inner belief systems and they choose not to 'see' what others believe outside of their 'belief circle.'

They gather together in groups who carry the same belief systems as they do to strengthen the views and opinions of their stories. They feel this gives them a sense of greater strength, inner power and security.

However, we ask you is this based on a false security or a true security?

We ask you this because to find your inner truth is to find your inner beliefs which are truth to you, which are precious to you.

We ask you to seriously consider these important points. For when you feel you are caught in views and fears of yourself and others, your spirit within cannot breathe. It cannot expand as you cannot find your truth when you carry pain and insecurity.

Once more the lesson is about self-love and looking deep within. How are your mirrors in your life? What is reflecting back to you? What guidance do you desire to have to allow greater reflections to come back to you?

All is an illusion in the Game of Play.

If you understand these great lessons, we say to you well done. If you have difficulty understanding, then please go back and read these lessons once again because here are many clues as to how to heal your life.

If you desired to host a party and invited people to your party, you would attract people with similar belief systems and similar energies. Who would be invited to your party? What would the rhythm be of the music? Would it be fearful or angry? Perhaps the rhythm would be too serious or heavy.

Or would the beat be inspiring, loving, kind, nurturing, wonderful and magical?

We encourage you to look within and to see your inner beat. Your inner beliefs set the beat of your life. To change the beat, means to look within and to see your truth.

Are you living in your heart, or are you living in your fear?

You are the masters of your own game. You set your own rules to your own universe. You set the laws to your own personal universe, and the law of the Great Universe allows you to discover your freedom of your choices.

Do you desire more pain and more fear? Or do you desire to heal?

When you desire to heal, then go back within your heart and listen to your heart.

The heart asks you, are you living in your integrity? Do you consider yourself to flow with truth from your heart? Or are you living with a false identity, as if you are hiding behind a mask?

To become strong within self and find your creator of love within you, your heart asks you to look within and to find if you are living in your own truth.

It is then that greater healing work can be done. It is then you will break through and learn to dance the Great Dance of Great Love. You will then learn to flow in the greater vibrations and learn to tune into the Great Love of the Universe.

You can have these blessings when you listen to your heart.

A Komo Ha Halima

Greetings, I AM AMMORAH

Pleiadian High Priestess on the Pleiadian High Council

Part 27: How do you dance in your life?

You are your own creators of your own lives and together you co-create your system, your world and the way it runs.

How does this reflect in your own life? You hold patterns within your energy centers created by the way you have been brought up by your teachers, your parents, your grandparents, your culture, your religion, your friends and family and your structure within your society.

Life will constantly reflect your inner pain and belief patterns back to you. When you feel the pain in your life, you are holding on to painful belief systems that will reflect back to you. These are the mirrors reflecting back to you constantly.

To learn to heal these painful belief systems and the pain you hold, it is important to learn to flow with love and to learn to let go of all your anger and your pain. It is then that greater reflections will come back to you.

Your belief patterns can be likened to your personal laws. In your society you have laws to follow and thus your society follows laws to keep everything in order.

Your belief patterns also work similarly within you. Your belief patterns have been programmed by you, and your belief patterns are like your 'internal laws.' Your internal laws desire to teach you what you have created, and thus your mirrors of illusion will reflect your internal laws back to you.

Your world is a reflection of your inner beliefs and of your universal play within your own universal system.

To find your belief patterns, or your 'internal laws,' look outside of you and feel them reflecting back to you like mirrors.

As you see these patterns occurring make a note of them and then look deeper within them. Where in your dance did they begin? What pain is it you need to let go of in order to beat the game?

Only you can discover this. Only you can feel this truth.

When you desire to change your reflection, you begin to look in your mirror deeper and into the cosmic spaces deeper. You begin to quieten your mind and look within your universal system. Where is it lacking love? Where have you not found yourself?

When you ask for light to assist you with clearing your painful ways in your life, it will always come to your assistance to help you with deeper reflection. Upon your discovery of what it is that needs to be released, light will always assist you to release your pain with Great Love.

You then learn to dance higher. Greater Light will come to allow you to celebrate and discover greater freedom.

Who are your guests at your private party for deeper reflection work for you to discover? Will you begin to seek people with higher energy waves? Will you seek to be with people who mirror your higher belief systems?

When you are ready you will be dancing higher together with others.

For a moment, we ask you to bring in Great Light and to be at peace. When you are in light, you only have light surrounding your beautiful self. We ask you to bring in Pleiadian Light Healers who are there to assist you in your healing work.

We are holding a space for your growth as we assist you in this work. We are then asking you to go deep within.

As you do this, we are opening a higher space for your learning and we will always assist you with this Divine Work. Thank your Pleiadian friends for helping you with these lessons and then release them with love when you have finished your work.

As you go about your play in your theatre, you will observe how your cosmic play is changing. People around you will become more positive and more forgiving because you are living in greater reflections of greatness.

The greater you allow your pain to be released, the greater the reflections will return to you. Learn this vital point of self-love. The greater you love yourself, and you begin to live in your heart with full integrity, the greater your life becomes.

Learn to live with greater love in your life.

Spiritual Strengthening
Building the flows of love

Exercise 11: Bring higher reflection to your life

1. Begin to relax with the deep breath in and out, slowly.

2. Bring in the Great Light and bring in your Angels and Pleiadian healers.

3. Breathe in light and breathe out light.

4. Imagine you are looking in a mirror. You are seeing the people around you who you are attracting. Can you see your friends? Can you see the people who relate to you often?

5. What belief patterns are they carrying? Are they similar to your own? Consider for a moment, in what way are they similar?

6. If the beliefs are not positive and healing for you, ask them to leave and to return as different people, filled with love and positivity.

7. Then, clear this mirror and only look at yourself as your beautiful self.

8. State firmly and clearly: 'I am now ready to allow my old belief patterns to go, whatever they were in my theatre of illusion of play.'

9. State firmly: 'I am now bringing in strength, positivity, love and healing.'

10. Thank all Light Beings who were present with you.

11. Slowly breathe in and out and relax.

12. Come back to your space slowly with the breath.

13. Always remember to be grateful for all the support we give you, to help you to grow towards your greater journey of love.

A Komo Ha Halima

Greetings, I AM AMMORAH

Pleiadian High Priestess on the Pleiadian High Council

Part 28: Creating peace together, how?

At this time, we as your Pleiadian Brothers and Sisters would like to invite you to our realm of existence.

We invite you to our realm of existence, to help you to see and understand greater plays and understand how we create, to help you expand your greater awareness and to help you learn 'collective love consciousness,' to create love and peace within your own realm.

At this time, in your space of time, you will learn much about the power of stepping into love together. It is in these spaces of being together, with one thought and one desire, you will learn to bring about great change.

In this lesson, we as your Pleiadian healers of Great Light, would like to demonstrate to you how we play and how we create. We would encourage you to take these next few pages slowly and perhaps read them again and again, until you begin to grasp the importance of being together with one thought collectively.

We are inviting you into one of our Divine Sacred Temples. You are invited to be with us as we are discussing together sacred purposes of understanding Divine Love.

In our realm, Pleiadian people are filled with deep spiritual love for each other. There are about twenty spiritually evolved Pleiadians presently sitting together in a circle.

We first greet each other telepathically and bond to each other with our sacred hearts. We feel this is important because we are opening not only to bonds of love, but also open ourselves for greater understanding for divine advancement.

During our meetings we come to advance and to learn. Not to be angry and bicker but to advance. This is our main target and because all of us are in line with Higher Will, we anchor Love within our being.

Because we understand how important it is to be in a group to advance together, we achieve greatly.

At this time of our gathering, we are discussing how we can help bring greater instruction to your planet because you require our assistance in a particular area.

We discuss this with our minds and bring our collective thoughts to the center into a portal of light. We see this happening within our minds and each one of us contributes our feelings and understandings telepathically.

We ask the Great Light to bring our ideas together and work on a greater outcome that we perhaps may not have yet discovered.

We then discuss these outcomes and come together with guidelines, which always benefit us greatly as well as the issue involved.

We then walk together to the great room of telecommunication and focus with our great minds on the planet we are targeting. We then send instructions and frequencies via our mind to those ones who are open to receive them, so they can receive it through the tele-portal dimension at the right time.

To you, this may seem as you would say perhaps, 'Far out.'

We understand you cannot do this at this time. We are pointing out that this is where you could be heading towards if you desired to do this. We are simply showing you the way that all this is very possible within your existence as well.

It is about learning to open your hearts with love and understanding.

We listen to one another with an open heart. We greet each other with an open heart. We love each other with an open heart.

There are those of us as 'Elder' Pleiadians who are far more advanced than many other Pleiadians and yet we, as advanced leaders, do not see ourselves as more important than the younger ones because we are all part of the Great Light, growing together and learning from each other.

This learning is vital for you. Do you not understand that you are from the same Great Light as us? Do you not understand that no one is more important than another and that you are, on your plane together, serving each other's needs?

For each one carries an important gift and that gift helps many other people advance.

Please consider this our dear Family of Light. If all what we say is true, you have a long way to go to reach these greater ways of existence.

However, we have shown you what is ahead. We have shown you the path to help you return to these greater ways.

Why do I say return? It is because you have already experienced all these ways in ancient times. You simply forgot how to do it. We are here to remind you and to help you understand you are playing the Dance in the Cosmic Light. You are invited to play along with us.

A Komo Ha Halima, I AM AMMORAH. We are your Tutors of Light, guiding you back to your precious gifts within.

A Komo Ha Halima

Greetings, I AM AMMORAH

Pleiadian High Priestess on the Pleiadian High Council

Part 29: Learning to work together

To learn to flow in the Greater Light and play in the love energies to create a greater life for you we, as your Pleiadian Tutors, would like to help you grasp deeper ways of love and flow for your greater blessings and for peace.

You have learned much already. Here, we take the opportunity to review a few lessons with you to give you a deeper understanding of what we have taught you through these pages before we carry on to greater lessons.

We hope you are enjoying these lessons for they give you much to consider. You have learned:

💜 Much about your Creators and the way they created you.

💜 Much about the cosmic dances and how you are learning to play higher in these times of your awakening.

💜 About the power of your energy body and your thought-power.

💜 How your health, vitality and creating a higher life are to do with the voltages you play and dance with.

♥ In order to create change within your society, you must come together because you hold the power of creation together.

In the future, many will desire this expansive knowledge. These ways we teach you are the keys to bringing change upon your plane collectively.

Energy has always been a part of your play through all your dimensional plays and lifetime dances. In your past history you were ignorant and played in the illusions that you and others had created together. You learned to create suffering and greatness together.

Now that you are awakening, you are able to learn how to transform energies into love and how to play in higher energies.

Before we discuss our next lesson to help you progress and move forward, we want to congratulate you for coming to this important stage.

You have learned much and now you are learning how to advance. You must congratulate yourselves and understand we appreciate you. You must appreciate yourselves because as you have already learned, self-respect increases your flows of power. All flows of existence and eternal power are within you.

You are part of all of creation and all of creation is a part of you. You are part of eternal life and eternal life is a part of you.

Nothing in your world is fixed. It is all a part of flow and all is a part of divine energy. The greater your discovery of your illusions, the greater your understanding of learning to transform energy becomes to develop greater energies to evolve towards higher ways of existence.

A Komo Ha Halima, I AM AMMORAH, Pleiadian High Priestess. We are your Healing Guides in the Light guiding you to your journey in the Great Light.

A Komo Ha Halima

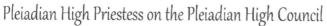

Greetings, I AM AMMORAH

Pleiadian High Priestess on the Pleiadian High Council

Part 30: Life is far greater than it seems

In the cosmic spaces of energy, you live in many different frequencies. Your frequency range increases as you learn about higher frequencies and higher learning.

Only a few decades ago, this information would have not been broadly broadcasted as the great majority of people were not ready to hear yet. You were discovering new angles of life and not yet awakening to the Truth within the Great Light.

Slowly, more and more heard the calling and began to open their hearts. The greater the amount of people opening their hearts, the more information could flood the earth.

Working in harmony collectively in large groups is vital at this stage in your evolution and in your play.

It is not about individual growth any longer. When we say this, the individual growth is vital, but we are turning our attention now to the collective consciousness because together, you will bring change to your plane.

You must wake up more each and every day to what is happening on your plane in order to find how you can play a great part in the change that will happen and is already happening on many levels.

You are in plays of greatness. You are now in a time when you will set your own rules. You will turn away from the rules which have been set by your leaders and learn to walk a higher way instead.

How can you do this you may ask? How can you, as a group of people with higher consciousness, bring about this incredible change?

It always begins with self. It begins with understanding how you are changing during the Great Awakening.

Many people on your plane, who are awakening, enjoy gathering in groups to talk about these cosmic changes. However, in doing those fine works they often forget about themselves. They constantly help others and guide others and work hard in the light.

The greatest work that needs to be done is within your own universal play first. Always look within before you look outside, for if you do not you will grow impatient and become frustrated.

Frustration and impatience do not flow with love energies. You must be patient, for this change will take time and it will take a great deal of effort.

Always look within. How are you playing in your own cosmic party? Are you filled with love? Are you filled with inspiration? Do you take time out to inspire yourself? Do you take time out to become fulfilled within? Or do you always seek change outside of yourself? Do you expect more of others than they can give at this time?

Many of you, who desire change and can grasp this higher information, can often become overeager and perhaps 'pushy' towards others to change their cosmic party rules to dance to your rhythm.

Light is never pushy. Light is always willing to take the time and patience for change. However, light also has a time-schedule but it always desires to have everyone at the Cosmic Play of Light to discover self, to evolve and become greater love.

To awaken your creator within, examination of self is crucial. We like you to consider these points please, to awaken your heart deeper.

Are you critical of yourself and of others? If you are, your individual Cosmic Play will not be able to play its highest magical tune. The tune of magic is love and it will only respond to love.

Are you angry with your past? If you are, your Cosmic Plays will not be able to awaken to their greatest until you let go and forgive all your past pain.

Are you fearful? If you are, how can you step into your creator self? How can you learn to play higher when you feel afraid? Learn to have courage to play higher.

You are all working here in a Universal Play together. No one is left out. However, some arrive at the Great Cosmic Party earlier than others.

Everyone is invited. Everyone has a party invite to join the love.

A Komo Ha Halima, I AM AMMORAH, Pleiadian High Priestess, guiding you to the Great Cosmic Party.

A Komo Ha Halima

Greetings, I AM AMMORAH

Pleiadian High Priestess on the Pleiadian High Council

Part 31: Coming together in greater plays of Cosmic Light

When you come together to play higher, we invite you to call us as Pleiadian Partners of Light inside of your circles. We can do much to help you create greater portals of light within your circle.

We ask you at these plays to be light-hearted and to have fun with the play of energies. We ask you not to take it too seriously as when you do, you will not be able to reach the higher dimensions. The higher dimensions are light and joyful.

Greet each other with deep love and respect. Acknowledging each other as from light is very important as it shows respect and you reflect your wisdom towards each other.

Always show love to each other and never criticize. Some of you in groups may be more experienced, but others catch up quickly when a strong leader is in the group. The leader must always respect his (or her) students because they are as important as the teacher. The teacher is never more important than the student. The students will become the teacher as they climb higher in the cosmic experiences of love.

Continuously express the love of each other. Why are they there? What would they like to achieve? How can you help them with greater growth?

As everyone in the group expresses their own love to others, greater reflection will take place. At times these reflections may be moments of deep soul-reflection as deeper aspects will become apparent.

As a group, why not set an intention with each other. When you desire to change the world together, you can set an intention together to bring change to a certain aspect.

Say prayers together and bring in the Archangels of the Great Light. Always bring in the Great Love of the Holy Violet Flame for transmutation to bring healing, balance and love into the circle.

All are encouraged to visualize a great portal as then a great portal of love will open. Visualize and sense your hearts opening to create greatness within yourselves and feel this space opening.

Place your intentions and visions within the portal and allow it to become greater. Feel and sense the energies change within the portal. Allow it to be there for some time and then allow it to close by thanking all the Beings of Love for allowing the portal to be created.

Afterwards take a deep breath in and out and allow the energies to settle.

It is important to discuss your experiences as a group to allow deeper reflection to take place.

Congratulate each other with this important group work together.

A Komo Ha Halima, I AM AMMORAH, Pleiadian High Priestess. We are guiding you to work together to bring change upon your plane.

A Komo Ha Halima

Greetings, I AM AMMORAH

Pleiadian High Priestess on the Pleiadian High Council

Part 32: Open a portal for love

As you have already discovered, you exist in whirlpools of energies, each holds unique frequency patterns. There are no two frequencies alike. They all hold a unique, individual coding. They hold a force within to create change.

When you tune into a particular desire with a clear intention, you create particular frequencies. These frequencies merge together to allow healing to take place within that boundary of clear intention.

For instance, if you tap into the frequency of peace, this frequency will override the frequency of war as frequencies will always work with opposing frequencies, depending on which one is stronger.

If enough people tuned into peace, you would overcome war and anger. Hence, you can come together as individuals and come together collectively.

To achieve greatness together, it takes a great deal of love. Love is the key to your higher advancement. You cannot reach these greater levels of advancement if unity is not present with each other.

Why is this so? It is because when you grow together, and you advance with each other to this greater and deeper way of love, you begin to understand the importance of unity.

When greater unity is created with great love, a higher dimension of play is opened. Its frequency within that higher dimension begins to tune itself into the sacred hearts of the people.

You create this frequency together as a group. This is because this frequency is created from your sacred hearts together. This frequency has a tremendous amount of love within and it shines in the sacred hearts collectively.

To create higher plays of love collectively, is to stand united in the same thought process together. Together you are able to create Sacred Portals of love and of peace.

When you desire to bring peace and love together as a group like this, you create an enormous strength not only for you as individuals, but also for the world.

Before you work this play, all must be united and clear with the same purpose. Already your sacred eye is working hard to bring this energy into existence when you are clear with one purpose.

Harmony is the greatest lesson here. Working together with the power of your sacred hearts, with the harmony of your desires is incredibly powerful.

When you do this, a great portal is opening when the information flows from the sacred heart to the crown and into the higher chakras collectively.

You are seeing the greater picture together, thus the closeness and the love within your group grows. When this happens, the creation force field within the group grows dramatically. Your thought-power and your thought-mastery will also increase during these processes.

You must all come together with perfect focus and dedication to create this portal of deeper understanding. If it is unbalanced because members of the group do not hold the focus, the portal will not open to its great potential.

However, this learning has greatly helped you evolve with higher spiritual abilities.

We encourage you to keep trying. Your blessings will be enormous upon achieving this grand love together.

When you come together as a group, desiring love and peace upon your plane, all must focus upon the same purpose.

Therefore, if you desire to create a loving group with the intention of opening up to higher understanding for the advancement and love of your human race, you must all come together with the understanding that all in the group must come from a heart of love and come together with one purpose only. That purpose is to dedicate your lives to the Great Light for the advancement of humanity.

You must come together often and create a love for yourselves, shining your sacred hearts of light towards each other and speak of only loving words. You must constantly live with the focus of love within yourselves. Then you will learn to open to the Greater Portals of Love.

At this time in your existence, this advanced knowledge may be too difficult for you to grasp. Please do not be discouraged in any way for we are showing the greater ways to create love and peace upon your plane.

We are encouraging you to come together often and practice.

If you desire humanity to change, if you desire to change your world to a world of peace and love, you must learn to come together and learn to appreciate each other. You must create a space of higher learning together and learn to accept each other.

Then you can create greater visions of love together. Then you can create a greater space for learning and for creating. Then you can create greatness together.

Whenever you do this portal frequency exploration work, you are building the same frequencies within yourselves also. This work will allow you to set higher cosmic laws in your own universal system within you, to create astonishing growth in your own lives. Your beliefs of life will become greater and you will receive many blessings of greatness.

Well done for your tremendous accomplishment. We praise your efforts. We welcome you back soon.

A Komo Ha Halima, Greetings, I AM AMMORAH. I am a guide here for you, guiding you back to your higher spiritual existence.

Spiritual Strengthening
Building the flows of love

Exercise 12: Open a great portal of love together

The goal is to open a portal of love for humanity upon your plane. During your practice exercises, you will evolve spiritually. Keep practicing. When you advance to the stage of being able to open the portal together, you will know when it has.

1. Before you begin in meditation, discuss together with a clear intention one aspect you wish to change upon your earth. You must all be in agreement with each other and have appreciation for each other. Discuss your images and draw this energy into your sacred eye together. You can do this with your imagination and focus.

2. Once you are in firm agreement, begin by relaxing together. We ask you to surround yourselves with the Great Light of the Angelic Realms and also ask us, your Pleiadian healers of light to be with you. We will keep this vision for you.

3. Breathe in and out slowly. If you can breathe together to a similar pattern it would be greatly advantageous.

4. Practice opening your heart, sharing your love with others in the group. Send telepathic messages of love. You will feel each other's love and you will enjoy the vibration of love together.

5. Imagine a Great Light opening in the middle of the circle. This light is there for you to use, to allow you to build up energy for the portal of Love you will create.

6. While you are breathing in the love energies, visualize the grand vision you have as a group together and place this vision with your sacred eye into the center of the group by directing the energy there and holding it. Constantly focus upon it.

7. Pour in the love from your sacred heart by feeling your love expanding and then direct your heart energy towards the light into the center.

8. When all are in unison together and all hold this great love together, you will feel this energy building and it will open into a gateway, a portal of great love.

9. Hold it as long as you can and then slowly let go. You will feel the energy building and it will open into a gateway, a portal of great love.

10. Hold it as long as you can and then slowly let go. You will feel the energy slowly being released.

11. Thank all Light Beings for supporting you in your important work.

A Komo Ha Halima

Greetings, I AM AMMORAH

Pleiadian High Priestess on the Pleiadian High Council

Part 33: Understand the power within to create change upon your plane

Imagine if you stood as one in groups together around the world, not only with one or two groups but with thousands of groups, all united with one thought, with one purpose.

The energies would certainly change upon your plane because the grandness you hold within your visions within these groups would become alive with love.

Energy, when it is infused with intention, becomes a living energy. Living energy moves and expands.

When energy is created with the love of your sacred hearts and when the vision within your sacred eye is strong with desire, together with your inner fire burning with intense yearning to bring change, you bring change upon your plane.

You have always been the creators of your energies upon your plane, but now it is for you to bring love and peace upon your plane.

The great question being asked at this moment is; 'How much do you desire to have a loving earth? How much do you want this for you, for your children and for generations to come?'

Begin to realize it is your choice. It is when you begin to understand you have this choice, you will move towards bringing it in. You are not on your own, for when you work with these powerful processes, you have many helpers working along with you.

It is your decision.

Learn to love every part of yourself and learn to love each other. Learn to appreciate your planet and learn to claim it back.

Claim back your beautiful earth and claim back your abundance. Claim yourselves back. Learn to work together and learn to bring peace and love.

When you see these things happening, be more determined to bring it in. Always thank Spirit for allowing this to happen.

It is your time to realize the power is within you to bring the change needed to your plane.

Creators, awaken the energies within you and understand the power you have in the cosmic play.

You have the keys to create change.

A Komo Ha Halima, I AM AMMORAH, Pleiadian High Priestess. We as your Pleiadian Healers are here to support your growth and healing.

Bring your vision alive

Your vision becomes alive,

when you bring it into your being.

Within you are gateways,

to create your dreams,

to bring them into existence.

Become aware of yourself,

of your energy,

of your passion,

of your strength.

You will then begin to understand,

your internal power.

A Komo Ha Halima

Greetings, I AM AMMORAH

Pleiadian High Priestess on the Pleiadian High Council

Part 34: Building your energy framework with strength

To build your dreams and your desires, you must realize the importance of building strength within your energy framework.

The greater your energy force field becomes, the greater your health, your outlook on your life, your abundance, your love and your dreams become.

Especially at this time of the Great Awakening when you are being asked to build peace and love in your world you require this great strength. Without strength you cannot begin to understand how to work with your energy.

Here you are learning to build upon your foundation of your energy framework. Before you create a building, you must have plans and you must have a strong foundation.

Your strength foundation is about understanding how to build your energy framework and how to keep your energy strong.

Imagine if you defended an incredibly important field of gold. What would you do? You would build high fences, structurally sound and you would make sure that every inch of that fence was guarded so that nothing could weaken this field to allow a thief to come in and take the gold away.

You would also want to make this field so secure that nothing that is of great value could escape this boundary you have created.

Your energy field is worth more than a field of gold. Your energy field is a rich resource of all possibilities of all your possible creations.

When you become aware of the vastness and the importance of your energy field, you will desire to protect it with all your might.

For the wise ones who understand this, they will desire to learn to protect it. They will desire to learn to understand how to strengthen it and how to stop energy escaping from their energy field.

When you have pain your energy is escaping. You must be in touch with your emotions and understand your pain.

Where is the pain you are holding? Do you long for the past? Are you in fear of the future? Is your anger creating weakness within your energy field?

When you are angry, your energy becomes depleted. Where your attention is, so your energy flows towards that direction.

Energy is always in movement. It dances with you. It can expand, grow in love, or shrink with pain.

Each one is constantly dancing with each other. When you desire to strengthen your energy field, strengthen your energy field by being in the light of your Angels.

When you are in the light and in the quiet, you are strengthening your energy field. When you forgive and release you are strengthening your energy field. When you love all of life and who you are and truly appreciate all things given from above, you are growing and strengthening. You are filling yourself with power.

The greater your experience of love and respect for your life becomes, the greater your strength. Allow all your pain to be released and always examine how to build the power within your energy frame work.

We wish to encourage you to do this following exercise to build your inner strength and to allow yourself to build a stronger energy field.

A Komo Ha Halima, I AM AMMORAH, Pleiadian High Priestess. We are here to support your journey upwards. We desire all of mankind to shift upwards. Are you ready to shift deeper into your heart of love?

Spiritual Strengthening
Building the flows of love

Exercise 13: Build a strong force field

We will place a special flame in your arena of play for greater strength.

1. Simply by breathing in and out the flames of love, your strength will greatly increase.

2. We ask you to visualize a sun and we would ask you to pull the sun into your solar plexus chakra gateway for greater strength by breathing in and out slowly.

3. Your solar plexus chakra is located near a main chakra gateway that leads to higher gateways of your greater bodies of light.

4. When you balance this chakra, you will bring into balance your other main chakras. The greater this chakra becomes in balance, the greater your inner strength becomes.

5. Simply breathe it in and breathe it out, allowing this chakra to expand and create greater strength within you.

Hold your own power

Every day from this day onwards,

be determined,

to bring in universal love.

Strengthen your sacred sun.

Be strong,

to hold your own power.

Refuse to give your power,

away to others,

instead,

use it for the love of life,

use it for love,

wisdom,

healing,

then your days will be,

forever blessed.

A Komo Ha Halima

Greetings, I AM AMMORAH

Pleiadian High Priestess on the Pleiadian High Council

Part 35: Your willpower

To play in higher cosmic energies, it is vital for you to find great portals of inner self willpower to play in these higher theatre plays.

These teachings may be difficult for you to grasp. We encourage you to read this information and to ponder upon it because it will help you to grasp your life greater.

Many on your plane have little or limited willpower. You have lost your strength because you feel you are not strong enough to carry on with your life with strength.

You give up your dreams easily and thus you create great drama plays of uncertainty and great fears. Your anger becomes greater because you give up on yourselves.

You may become envious of those who have greater willpower than you because you see them succeeding in life and their whole 'life' play is a mystery to you. You wonder how some play their game and succeed, yet others have great difficulty with success.

As Pleiadians we enjoy playing with our inner portals of strength. We call them portals because they are portals of energy. They can spin greater and smaller, depending on the energy that is placed within the play of strength.

You understand from our teachings that everything is an illusion. You live in illusions and you create your 'realities' from your illusions. You are living in an illusional self, desiring to expand and to grow and to understand deeper self.

You are living in mirror 'realities.' Each mirror reflects a different 'reality' back to you in the Dance of Light.

You think your life is 'real' upon your plane at this time and you believe you truly exist upon your plane.

However, in 'reality' you are not truly on your plane at all. Your presence upon your plane is created with the illusion for the purpose for your higher learning and higher expansion as your Higher Being.

Because you believe your life to be truly 'real,' you live in the play of a 'real' world.

You are strong beings and it is time to begin to find the strength within you.

When you play higher in the cosmic experiences of the mirror illusions, you must understand that your inner willpower holds a great key for discovering your creator within.

Prime Creator is powerful and strong. It exists eternally and it is Almighty. It is eternal force and its flames burn eternally in the magic of the mirror of eternal existence.

You are a part of that eternal force. You hold your magical mirror of your 'reality' to discover your creator within you because everything is part of Creator Existence, including you.

Because Prime Creator is powerful and strong, you are powerful and strong also when you discover this within you. You hold incredible gifts waiting to be discovered by you.

Some of you have developed your inner strength well. You hold a deep presence and a knowing. Your heart guides you to your path with deep knowing and so your success is great.

Why is success great with your creator-found strength?

It is because this energy is what creates success. This strength is what creates power. In essence it is what creates your significant creator-self force. It is what creates new portals. It is creation, force, magnificent, magnetic, power, strength.

This is the power of inner strength when it is played within the Cosmic Forces of Light. When this power of strength is directed with great clarity, fueled with love, it creates more power and love.

At this time, only relatively few people have discovered this inner great force upon your plane. Many others will find it difficult to comprehend and even accept it is there to be found.

Many become envious and even angry of the ones who have found it.

We go back to the mirror of 'realities.' If envy and anger are within your being and they mirror pain back towards you in your life, perhaps some deeper reflection work needs to be done to help you become free from deeper belief systems of your pain.

Always forgive all your pain. Allow it to go from within you. Learn to heal greater in the love.

A Komo Ha Halima, we are here to guide you to your greatness and to help you discover how to flow with greatness.

A Komo Ha Halima

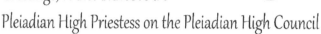

Greetings, I AM AMMORAH

Pleiadian High Priestess on the Pleiadian High Council

Part 36: Understanding the play of thought

Thought is not only a 'thought,' but a play. Every thought you carry out during your day has some affect within your life. Some thoughts carry greater frequencies and they will do more for you than other thoughts.

The greater the love frequencies held within your thoughts, the less the negative can play out as love will always nullify denser frequencies.

Love is a force and it will always remain a force. Love grows. It is not simply there and stays the same over time. Love is a force that expands and will always keep expanding.

When you as people bring in love together, the force of love becomes greater and nullifies the lower, denser energies which have ultimately been created by belief forms and thought-power.

When you bring in the love, your greater visions allow a more powerful energy to come upon your plane to bring great change. This great change will eliminate all pain that has been caused by beings, who had, and still have, visions of your pain and fear, because they desired to have you in realms of energies in lower existence of pain.

These beings of great defiance are also strong with their thoughts, power and desire. Their visions of pain and fear for your 'real' experience allows you to believe that this is all there is to life.

You carry out their thoughts and they become your thoughts and thus you create a circle of pain. Once the circle has been created it is difficult to step out of the circle.

Dear ones, we say to you, your pain and anger on your plane is all an illusion.

The 'reality' is that you can free yourselves from it.

Your Love thought-power together as one, standing united, will fight against the illusion created by beings of great defiance. You will then bring about change together, standing together with one thought and one love. Together you create strength and change.

We say to you, learn to play higher at the Cosmic Party and you will break the chain of pain. You will then sing the same song and play the same beat with harmony.

By coming together and having visions together of Love and creating portals of Love with great intention, you will break the patterns of pain and anger.

At first, because many of you do not believe and understand, the energy will not be strong enough to stop large quantities of pain upon your earth.

However, as you see small changes taking place, you will see this work as incredibly important. It is then you will learn to grow into it.

Learning to grow into new energy work is vital for your spiritual growth. It is not only about the individual any longer. Now you are stepping into greater work collectively.

Many lifetimes you desired to do this Divine Work. You searched for ways to heal your people and your earth but it was not the time yet to step into this great work. The powers of your creator energies had not opened yet.

You still had some work to do before these times arrived. These times have arrived now and many people upon your plane are already doing this sacred work, preparing for the great work ahead.

A Komo Ha Halima. I AM AMMORAH. I have a great deal of love for you, and hence I desire to be part of your new creation consciousness. Will you listen? Will you open your heart to the greater love?

Creating your dreams

To create your dreams,

what does it take?

Love, strength, great wisdom,

reflection from within.

To find greatness within you,

is to find strength within you,

to give you the determination,

and the understanding,

that everything is already yours to have.

It is time to believe it.

It is time to step into it.

When you do,

it will be yours to have.

A Komo Ha Halima

Greetings, 1 AM AMMORAH

Pleiadian High Priestess on the Pleiadian High Council

Part 37: Finding greater love for each other

In your world some of you play a higher tune and others play a tune not so high. It is easy for people to find themselves in a battle against each other on an energetic level as to who plays what tune finer than another.

At this time of the Greater Party of Cosmic Light, it is important you learn to come together in unity, accepting each other in unity in this Great Dance of Light.

It is time to finish all your pettiness of who is accepting this and who is accepting that because it is not your usual, 'Universal Standard,' within your own mirror of 'realities.'

It is time to embrace each other and to embrace each other's gifts because you are all invited to the Greater Dance. However, you cannot dance the Greater Dance until you learn to have peace and love for each other.

You are all playing on magnificent levels and the greater you learn to play with these energy forces of creation within you, the stronger you become. It then becomes vital to tune into the love rather than the anger or the envy.

Your powers are growing when you grow within your love. You must remember not to fight against your brothers and sisters, especially when your inner powers are growing, because as your light expands, your responsibilities also become greater.

You must accept each other. Together you must learn to dance the Cosmic Flows of Life, for if you do not, forces will be fighting in opposition, like they have in your past.

All people in your dimension came here to dance higher together. You loved each other so much in the plays of light that together you desired to create a platform for higher light to bring Great Love to the lower dimensions.

To be able to achieve this magnificence, it is important to stop the small plays of envy, to stop the small plays of who is better, who is leading who, who is a greater light worker and who is a greater healer.

All people are playing in the same cosmic field together, each reflecting different 'realities' to each other to learn from, to embrace, to create and to become greater.

You are all awakening to the magnificence within you. Embrace this warmth and enjoy the desires of desiring more. Feel your love within growing more each day.

Feel the greatness of who you are. Stop dwelling on your pain. Stop dwelling on your past and what you were subjected to.

Embrace the moment and embrace your life. Fill each other with your love and positivity. Forgive those who are not positive. Forgive them and be in the love. Turn the energies from negative to positive. You have the power to do this. You are finding the creator within you. Embrace your inner power.

Allow your inner power to grow to become great. Allow it to show.

Allow the creator force within you to show. Allow it to evolve. Connect with its very being and allow it to grow.

A Komo Ha Halima, our warmest love to you. We are your Pleiadian Healers teaching you to let go and to heal in the light.

A Komo Ha Halima

Greetings, I AM AMMORAH

Pleiadian High Priestess on the Pleiadian High Council

Part 38: Learning to create love 'realities'

As we have already discussed with you, energies are at play in every moment. Force is energy and the greater the clarity of thought-power is used in conjunction with a particular energy of a desire; that particular force strengthens. This force you have created then becomes your 'reality' to experience as it allows itself to show in your life.

As you are rising in the Cosmic Creation of Light, you are discovering much. You are finding what strengthens and enhances your own gifts and power. You are also discovering what weakens your energy field.

Each creation has significant deeper levels of lessons to discover. All lessons in the dimensional play have deeper reflections to consider.

Evolution always moves forward. It always learns and discovers. It always pushes onward for greater expansion and love.

We ask you to evolve into greater expansion. We ask you to always find greater ways of evolving your greater gifts, to enhance your own lives and to enhance each other's life.

You are a miracle of energy force within yourself. This is because of the strength of the creator force within you. You have creator force within you and this force becomes stronger when you focus upon it.

Your spirit is part of the creator force, though not the same. This may confuse you. The spirit is alive and has a personality. The creator force gives the spirit power to exist, and thus they work united as one, and they work together to create and to enhance your life.

Your spirit and creator force combined desire you to expand in your work of life experiences and to understand your truth of who you are.

They up the game of life when you are ready to. They are patient and are happy to wait until you are ready to receive the invitation.

They are eternal and as far as they are concerned, no time exists in the play of life to dance together.

Your life is incredibly important. Each lifetime you come to your plane you discover more about self. In some lifetimes you learned not to work so hard and in others, perhaps about working harder.

Every lifetime has strengths and goals. Each lifetime is important for balancing the scale of energies.

How are you living this lifetime? Can you feel changes happening in this lifetime?

Many of you are now in a time to balance the scale of love. In past lifetimes you loved, and you knew the power of love and creation and in many other lifetimes you learned the gift of losing love. You learned to distrust yourself and others. You learned to have pain and you discovered anger.

When you discover anger and pain in your life it does not mean you are not evolving, for great evolution also happens when you learn to transform your pain into your joy. Also learning to forgive yourselves and each other are vital spiritual lessons of growth.

Many people turn to the Great Light because of their inner suffering and they desire to understand how to free themselves from the pain.

Indeed, the past was a time to understand these strong, dense emotions and feelings, to allow you to evolve and come to a greater understanding about choices in life. Which way would you choose to live; in the love, or in the anger, fear and in pain?

For those of you who desire to step into the greater energies of love at this time, you are being asked that same question.

Which do you prefer to play in? Do you choose the anger, the pain and fear? Or do you choose to play in love energies?

The choice seems simple in your existence of play, but the answer is far from simple. You have learned much on your path. You have experienced both 'light' and 'dark' and you have come to believe everything around you is 'real' and that everyone carries 'real' issues with them and that your issues are 'real' and that you have 'real' situations around you that can make you angry, fearful and in pain.

It is easier to walk in the mirror of love, because in these higher cosmic plays, only love returns to you because all mirrors reflect back to you your inner beliefs. But how can you experience this love 'reality?'

Your choice becomes your 'reality.' It becomes your experience to have.

However, if you have not chosen yet you will not understand this lesson. It will not come to you until you begin to choose to experience it.

This is a time for deep reflection work.

How much do you desire to experience love? How much do you desire to understand your inner power to create greater love 'realities?' How much do you desire to understand your magical mirror to reflect greater love back to you in your Cosmic Spaces of Dance?

This can only be answered by you, as you have the answer. You are your own creators and law makers of your universal energies. You set your own rules. Reflection follows your rules.

You may consider this and decide you have had enough of the anger, fear and pain. But having had enough is not sufficient to dance higher in the rays of Cosmic Love.

What does it truly take? What does it truly take to draw away from the anger, fear and pain?

Greetings, our warmest love from the Pleiadians and all Star Beings of Love who love you, and desire you to return to the highest love dimensions where we can dance together in the peace, love and harmony. I AM AMMORAH, Pleiadian High Priestess on the Pleiadian High Council.

A Komo Ha Halima

Greetings, I AM AMMORAH

Pleiadian High Priestess on the Pleiadian High Council

Part 39: The wheel of energy keeps turning

Your world is created within a reflection of a reflection. In itself are many different dimensions of play. Each has different lessons and experiences to choose from. Each has different outcomes depending on how the game is played.

You are in a game of a maze of entanglement. How will you find the Portal of Love to experience higher love? How will you stay away from the simpler road of anger, pain and fear?

Anger, pain and fear will always look attractive until you become fully grounded in the love dimensions.

You understand 'pain' dimensions well. These ways have become easy for you to experience as you have discovered it well and it has become a great part of you over many lifetimes.

The gate to anger, pain and fear is significantly large. It is wide and easy to find.

The love gate is narrow. It can only be found by those who consciously keep working towards this gate because they desire a greater outcome and desire a greater game of play.

What are the benefits of each of these gates?

The first gate, the gate of anger, pain and fear, is more attractive to the majority of people in your living 'reality' at this time because it is widely known and has been greatly discovered.

The energies of pain have been widely broadcasted everywhere and its energies are strong. It is infectious, well supported and well known.

It is a struggle not to be in these lower energies because your universal patterns have become accustomed to it.

These 'pain' energies have become 'settled' on your plane and thus it has become a struggle to reverse the energy wheel and turn it to the opposite direction.

Your energy body becomes accustomed to certain patterns. When you desire to change your internal programs, the old energy programs will fight the new and desired energy programs. Therefore, the fight to move the wheel of energy to the other side often proves to be difficult and can be enormously frustrating for you as the players.

Turning the wheel of energy play can be frightening to your ego as expectations are not yet known until the outcome is realized.

Your expectations run your wheel where ever it turns to. When you are in the 'pain' frequencies, your expectations of pain feed the turning of the wheel, thus the power to move it in the direction of deeper pain increases.

When you introduce another belief system into the energy mixture, your energies do not comprehend where it is 'settled' and they begin to stir. At times they can cause 'panic.'

As you can see, to choose another way of life may be challenging.

The gateway of love is more difficult to find and it takes a great deal of strength to find true love for all of life. It is a fight between the old patterns and the ways of love, but love is stronger and when the determination is to turn the wheel to love, love will always win.

The wheel turns to ways of love and life becomes easier. Life begins to fall into place.

However, the struggle to turn the wheel in the greater direction can be difficult.

Here is the energy play once again. When the wheel is turning comfortably to the direction of pain, and life begins to show the wheel higher ways of love, if the heart has not been awoken to love yet, the mind will struggle with love and it will desire to turn towards the old patterns of pain once again.

This is because the ego mind is comfortable with 'pain' patterns.

The mind battles against the energy of the heart, until the heart has finally won.

The mind in itself is an energy and it can hold you back from your game of play and your higher dance. The mind and the heart will not follow each other in sequence until the mind surrenders its play to the love of the sacred heart.

It is similar to two dance partners dancing together. When one hears one beat and the other hears the other, they are out of tune. One will take over from the other until the two begin to synchronize, until full balance is found to dance to the same beat.

Only then a beautiful harmonious dance is created.

Therefore, to win this game, to learn to dance the ways of love, to have total partnership and unison between the mind and the heart, one must completely surrender to the Game of Light.

A Komo Ha Halima, I AM AMMORAH, Pleiadian High Priestess, guiding you to create a greater love 'reality.'

Spiritual Strengthening
Building the flows of love

Exercise 14: Bringing the heart and mind together to work in unity

1. Begin to relax your body, breathing in deeply and breathing out deeply.

2. Feel your love for your heart.

3. Bring in the love from the Archangels and Divine Beings. Call them into your heart. Call in the Pleiadians in the light. Sense their presence.

4. See a big turning wheel in your mind's eye. See it turning more and more easily. Create a portal in your mind above the turning wheel and say the following:

5. 'My heart and my mind are at one. They are at one with each other. Both work together in union as a close partnership. They are both filled with love and their goal is to create love in my life. Forever this may be. Amen.'

6. Feel the wheel turning now harder and harder.

7. Slowly breathe in and out and feel this image leave.

8. As you do this on a regular basis you will understand your mind is growing with the heart to work in unison together. Your 'reality' will reflect a higher way of love, peace and happiness and inner power.

A Komo Ha Halima

Greetings, I AM AMMORAH

Pleiadian High Priestess on the Pleiadian High Council

Part 40: Learning the guidelines to open higher gateways

You are able to live in various dimensions on your plane. On your earth at this time you may assume each person is living in the same dimension as you are. After all, are you not all living on the same earth plane together?

This is the illusion. What is the 'reality?'

The great 'reality' is your plane is not as 'fixed' as you may think it is. Depending how you play the game depends on which energies play out in your life. You are in a play to learn how to climb out of your pain illusions into the greater plays of love.

Your game is to begin to understand your energies of illusions around you and learn to play a higher game. All of life is a game, regardless of the 'reality' you exist in and how you play in your 'realities.'

These are some guidelines to follow to help you open gateways to higher 'realities':

♥   Understand you play in energy illusions.

♥   You are living in a playground of energy.

♥ Every experience is a dimensional energy and it becomes stronger or weaker depending on what you focus upon.

♥ If you desire change, you must learn to bring it within your own force field first.

♥ If you desire change, you must look within to find your greater desires.

♥ If you desire to change the rules of your life, you must understand you are the creator and that anything is possible.

For those who are able to keep up with these guidelines, here is another guideline.

♥ Always understand the forces at play. Fear, anger and pain are part of denser energies on your plane. They are not real until you begin to focus upon them because you, individually and collectively, bring them into your 'reality' to play the game based upon those energies.

The strongest energy is the energy from your Prime Creator and your Creators and that is the force of Universal Love.

Love is able to nullify all denser energies but only when the player knows how to play with love because love also has different dimensions and gateways within itself.

It can work for the player and work against the player, depending on how the player sets the laws in his (or her) universal law system.

To learn this higher game, it takes time to absorb the lessons and then to learn to practice them in your own lives. The higher your game becomes, the greater your blessings become.

In the following lessons, you will learn how to find your incredible power. It is vital for you to learn how to play higher. To help you find the grandness and the creator within your being, it is vital for you to learn the game of illusion in order to make the right moves.

A Komo Ha Halima, I AM AMMORAH, Pleiadian Teacher and High Priestess, dwelling with you in eternal peace.

A Komo Ha Halima

Greetings, I AM AMMORAH

Pleiadian High Priestess on the Pleiadian High Council

Part 41: All is energy in your world

All in your world, all that happens upon your plane, is the result of an energy play.

These forces of energies are strong and can become more powerful depending on the greater plays of consciousness upon your plane.

When people focus upon something together, this can play out. These are the laws of Cosmic Flows. All is energy and depending on how skilled you are with sending your energy to your plane, with love, fear, anger, frustration, it is how it will play out.

Nothing in your life happens without a reason. A collision does not 'just' happen. You may not have caused it yourself, but how about if we brought out the lesson, collectively, you and the other party may have caused it together.

It will always play out in the same ways. Your 'illusion' will say it is not so, but energy will always play the same rules.

Forces of opposite sides can attract each other. If one side is weaker and the other is stronger, you both will come against each other in a collision. Opposite poles are always part of the game.

How can you avoid collisions of energies? This lesson takes deep reflective understanding.

This is a connection between you and energy, knowing you can have more control over your life than you realize.

Many light workers know this part of the game, but perhaps you do not understand the reason why it works. Thus, here is our lesson.

The universe is made of different energy flows. Universal Love, being the most powerful in the creation force of life, is Almighty, Powerful and Grand.

When you place 'white light' around a car, or plane, or your house and trust it and let it be, you are affectively borrowing light force field which is the protective field from the universal love flows, to protect the very items or people you value.

You are able to command it to happen because you are senders of energies.

Hence, protect yourself and your children and any other passengers before you travel. Always protect your car before travelling, protect your home and any other valuables you possess which are important to you.

Protect it with higher forces of love energies. Higher forces of energies repel lower forces of energies. By asking for the light to protect you and to surround you, your loved ones and your valuables, you are directing higher flows towards all you care so much for.

We hope you understand this lesson and see the importance of this play, for if you desire to enter the Great Cosmic Dance Party you need to become smarter with your ways.

You are not playing life little anymore. Now you are seeing how you can defend yourselves against lower forces.

Will you use them however? Will you smarten up?

We ask you to try if you have not yet already, and then observe. People who try new ways and observe are smart. Be smart energy workers and you will win the game.

A Komo Ha Halima. We are Pleiadian Guides and Tutors of Light, assisting you with finding your greatness and helping you to live a life filled with love.

Imagine peace on earth

Imagine a world,

where peace has been restored.

Imagine a world,

without pain or suffering.

Imagine a world,

with peace on earth,

children smiling,

with happiness,

feeling safe.

Learn to stand united,

and bring in the flows of love,

Together.

A Komo Ha Halima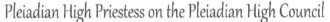

Greetings, I AM AMMORAH

Pleiadian High Priestess on the Pleiadian High Council

Part 42: Using your sacred eye to create your desires

You have already discovered how powerful your sacred eye is. Your sacred eye is a gateway to your creation.

Constantly you create with your sacred eye. A long, long time ago, you used this power-eye (as you called it then) with purpose and with greatness. You certainly understood the power of this portal.

Your sacred eye is a gateway to higher energy. When it is used correctly, you are able to see beyond the current situation and you are able to bring in desires and higher goals.

Because you have forgotten the power of the sacred eye gateway, you do not understand its value. You do not understand its potential. You do not recognize its great value.

Your sacred eye gateway constantly creates energy. It is constantly in motion creating your thought patterns and your inner beliefs. Combined with the energy of positive thought-power, the sacred eye center creates an energy cycle and energy waves of Cosmic Dances, dancing in unity to create a greater life for you.

These cosmic dances are encoded within your personal universal belief system. They carry out what they are instructed to do.

Imagine for a moment, you are a high-tech computer programmer. Not a learner, but a High Cosmic Computer Programmer. You have all your programs in synchronization and they work together smoothly. Each center sends an electrical force to another center and all is balanced and all work in harmony. Their timing is always perfect and the outcome is always predictable.

Welcome to your creator self. This is what you do constantly with your own programming. You are inputting data into your electrical circuits and your computer data will play out your illusions in your life, which you gather are 'real.'

You are constantly creating your life. You are constantly inputting data. These bits of data are mainly influenced by the way you see and perceive your life to be. You may think you are in pain and you believe your life to be painful and thus your life becomes more painful.

Or, you may be playing higher. You believe in success and you receive success. Thus, you create success.

What is your game? How is it working out within your universal belief system?

Each of you is connected to the larger Universe. Your sacred eye is connected to the Greater Portal of Life, to the forces of the Universal Energy Consciousness.

When you learn to tap into the Greater Universal Power with an Awakened Heart, with strong willpower, you create your life into a greater and more loving way.

Perhaps I am moving too quickly. Let us go back to some basic lessons.

Your sacred eye is a powerful chakra. It holds different frequencies of energy within it. When it is awakened, it can tune into higher energies which awaken this Light Gateway Path, and your life becomes more greatly awakened. You are able to see higher ways of life and you understand your life can change. You see the power and the beauty in life and you find great inspiration within yourself.

When this Light Gateway is not in tune with higher energies, it feels dull. Your life reflects the dull feeling and it becomes confused. It becomes uncertain of its purpose and it does not see its beauty. Hence, your life reflects this feeling. It may feel isolated from itself and separated because it is not recognized. Therefore, your life may also reflect this.

Your sacred eye can become more alive with energy and when it is alive and understands the sacred heart frequency well, they will sing together in harmony.

When the solar plexus region is well awakened, the solar plexus sends out stronger forces to the heart. Combined with the sacred eye, you have a powerful creation force to create your dreams.

Your sacred eye holds a deep magical tool within itself. It develops when it is used well and it is able to create incredible good. It is also able to be used for not so good purposes and when it is used for these purposes, it works against the flow of the universe. Thus, for the person who misuses this precious gift, their outcome is not blessed.

Cosmic laws state, these sacred areas must always be used for the purposes of love and healing only. When it is used for greatness it will be rewarded well and gateways of love will come streaming in towards this person.

Again, it is about your personal choice. You live in a world of freedom. It is your choice to use these techniques for healing and love for your life and others, or to control and manipulate others. It is up to you, but please be aware it will come back to you many times over depending on the choices you make.

We, as Evolved Enlightened Pleiadians desire to teach you the Great Love Way because it works and it is far more powerful than pain and anger.

We desire to help you find your inner creator in the most powerful ways possible.

A Komo Ha Halima, I AM AMMORAH, Pleiadian Teacher and High Priestess, dwelling with you in eternal peace.

A Komo Ha Halima

Greetings, I AM AMMORAH

Pleiadian High Priestess on the Pleiadian High Council

Part 43: Why you must train your sacred eye well

To use the sacred eye well, you must train it. When you have a puppy, you must train it also. The sacred eye must also be trained to become a powerful tool in your creation.

The sacred eye is trained by learning to control it.

Your sacred eye has a mind of its own when it is not controlled. It wonders off and decides its own rules, what is good and what is bad, depending on how you have created your belief systems of your own play.

You may not have been able to train it until now because you may not have realized the powerful relationship between the sacred eye and the thought.

Your visualization is controlled by your sacred eye. The stronger your visualization is, the stronger your sacred eye becomes.

You may say it is just 'imagination' within the mind. Where is this imagination then? How is it used? How has it been misused?

For what you think and visualize, will be created within your 'reality' with the power of your sacred eye.

Your thoughts direct these energies constantly to encode your personal universal system. When you focus upon something, you are inputting data to create your 'reality' of life.

You have been commanding your mind continuously to create codes for you to work with and to play with.

Your sacred eye is mainly powered up by your heart and the solar plexus. It is also powered up by your other chakra gateways. Many chakras you do not even know of at this time. They awaken at a later stage in your evolution and they help you to awaken to higher planes.

Your sacred eye is the commander, the processor as it were, of your wishes and your commands, powered up by the wishes and reflections of your heart.

Can you see from these teachings how important it is to train your sacred eye to become a portal of love?

This is why, when you play in these high energy games, you must always check in to see what your belief systems are by the way they reflect back into your life and then, if necessary, change them to help you grow into a higher way of love.

You must learn to train your sacred eye to bring in higher dreams and to help this area understand higher instruction.

This differs a little from some of your current understandings about bringing in dreams. Many people on your plane have been taught: to change your life you must change your thinking and then your life will flow.

This is true to an extent, because your thoughts carry an incredible power within themselves, but this is only part of the equation. Visualization is only part of the equation. Using love and joy, is only part of the equation.

To bring it together, to create a greater life, you must up your game and bring unity between your centers so that every center flows and communicates with each other.

Your solar plexus must be strong with internal fire and greater strength. It must love and only love and never criticize.

It must have a firm understanding this journey is yours and nothing else is as important as your journey. It must understand you are here to fulfill your sacred commitments and it will seek to bring you those sacred commitments.

Your heart must be flowing with love. A love that is pure and forgiving. A love that is joyful and kind. A love that is inspiring and grateful.

Your sacred eye must have a mind that is willing to play the game of love, flowing together with the strength and the fire of your fire chakra, together with the flow of the love chakra. They create a sea of dynamic energies, bursting forth in incredible life-force field energies of creation.

Can you feel the power and the greatness in these teachings? How do you find this incredible power? How do you find this incredible fire?

A Komo Ha Halima

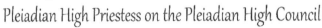

Greetings, I AM AMMORAH

Pleiadian High Priestess on the Pleiadian High Council

Part 44: Finding your inner power

Energies flow into each another. Each gives its own lesson of divinity and power. Each gives you lessons of balance and greater flow.

Each energy dances with another. It is like a perfect love dance flowing in and flowing out. The waters flow in and the waters flow out and the Rivers of Light flow in and the Rivers of Light flow out.

Your energy body flows like the waters of a river, gently and powerfully, all in greater pathways for deeper purpose and for greater love.

You are an incredible creation. When you discover your power, you can create magnificence between the flows of energies like a love dance, each following the other, each believing in each other, each holding a great trust with each other.

However, when the dance is not dancing to the perfect beat, when it is not dancing together in a love dance, when one flow is working in opposition to the other, the flows cannot perform their perfect, synchronized dance. It cannot then realize its potential of perfect balance.

These energy flows are felt in your 'reality' of life. When your Rivers of Light and energies of light dance together, you are in the flow of the light and all will come towards you flowingly, gently and powerfully, all in perfect alignment. Such is the balance of creation.

When we look at creation force itself, Prime Creator always flows in synchronization.

You are a small version of Prime Creator. Each of your energies within you dances together with a great performance of love. Each of your energies has rules with each other creating harmony, all working towards the greater purpose of love. When one energy flow works with the other, the others also work together.

Prime Creator also has energy centers and you are a part of all that is perfect, balanced and powerfully aligned. You are here to explore greater parts of your divinity and it desires more than anything for you to explore your creator within you, your beauty, your greatness and your love.

You are here to explore the very being of you. You are here to explore your inner beauty.

Throughout all your lifetimes on your earth plane, you forgot (by and large) all these truths. You pulled away from Divine Source and as a result you felt empty, insecure, not sure of your future. You forgot where to find sacred guidance and you forgot your inner greatness.

The Great Fire from your Prime Creator and your Creators was (in your discovery of pain) lost.

It is now you need to re-discover it, to find your greatness back once more.

Your solar plexus has been targeted for many tens of thousands of years. Because you lost your fire within, you pulled away from Divine Source and therefore your inner fire diminished.

When you find the source of creation within you once more, your fire will again burn steadily and it will allow the flow of life to return to your body. It will then give you an incredible love and energy for your greater purpose, as the strength of the fire gives deep purpose and understanding that the power of the Creator is within you and then you can find your greatness within.

When your solar plexus is small with its inner fire, just enough to keep you alive, your greater purpose is not truly felt. You exist from day to day with great numbness in life. You may feel as if the world is critical towards you and you are critical towards others.

This is because you do not feel you have enough firepower to light your own fire to fulfill your dreams. Thus, you take your attention away from your own dreams to a state of not knowing how to achieve your dreams.

You are and will feel like this until you begin to feel the firepower returning within you.

To fulfill your dreams, to allow your fire to become greater, you must become aware of your inner power and you must feel your own fire within. You must learn to find it for then you will become more fulfilled.

You must learn to love yourself and who you are and draw deep within you. You must find the source of your power and then claim it back and decide that no one will ever dim your fire again.

Many of you have been dimmed with your dreams because you felt no one believed in them or supported them, or somehow you lost the opportunity to dream big. Your dreams did not work out and you became dull within, without inspiration and without hope.

With these feelings, you forget your source of inner power and therefore you draw back from life. To find it once again will take understanding of what your source of inner power is, together with a deep desire and willpower.

Many people have forgotten about their firepower.

How do you find it once again?

A Komo Ha Halima, I AM AMMORAH, Pleiadian Teacher and High Priestess, dwelling with you in eternal peace.

A Komo Ha Halima

Greetings, I AM AMMORAH

Pleiadian High Priestess on the Pleiadian High Council

Part 45: You are connected to universal energy source

We have already explained your higher connection. First, it is an understanding it is there, and then it is about learning to claim it.

We have already given you the information earlier throughout these pages of drawing the spiritual sun into your solar plexus region. This region is the greatest chakra to concentrate on. This chakra keeps feeding you with energy to keep you alive and well.

The solar plexus is situated near a main cross highway of energy lines and greater chakra flows within your light body.

You are linked through these higher gateways directly to Source and Source feeds you constantly.

Imagine you are a part of a system that everything and everyone is connected to, a Universal Energy Source that keeps you alive and keeps you in the 'system' of learning and expansion.

You may have trouble with this idea; perhaps because you believe you are not connected to anything this large, or perhaps you believe you are only human and you have no larger self and no energy body to keep feeding into the system that is part of you.

If you were part of something so great, why would you not be constantly linked to it? If you could find the key to link into it deeper and into it greater, would you not desire this?

If you could link into this source that is so great, so powerful, so magnificent, to use it in your own life to feel nourished, become healed, experience the creator within, would you not desire to experience these dances in the Higher Light?

You are invited to join us in this Divine Light. Maybe it is difficult to follow this information because these teachings are far beyond the teachings you have been taught in general upon your earth plane.

Yes, you are part of a system that is so significant, so beautiful, so marvelous, so perfect and your creation of your being is perfect.

♥ Remember who you are and how magnificent you are and you will find your inner power.

♥ Remember to play in the dances of the light and your inner power will develop.

♥ Remember the light and the beauty within you and your inner beauty will build and the strength you will gain will be magnificent.

♥ Remember the beauty. Remember the love. Let go of all that has been of pain and step into a stronger self.

You are part of a creation that is beautiful. You are part of a creation force that is love, filled with desire to help you to grow in the light that you are.

Each day draw in the spiritual sun (with your intention) into your solar plexus region and this inner fire will spark up greater. You will then find your inner firepower. You will find your inner creator to create your life with magnificence.

You will find your glory within and the glory of who you are. You will find delight within your creation, and creation itself will be marvelous for you to discover.

Will you wine and dine with your creator energies? Will you celebrate with us, knowing you are discovering your inner powers? Will you dance to a tune that is higher and brighter than you have ever discovered in this life previously?

We are inviting you to our Cosmic Party of Love where all are dancing to a tune that is beautiful and filled with love.

A Komo Ha Halima, I AM AMMORAH. I am here as a Guide, helping you to grow to higher love consciousness.

A Komo Ha Halima

Greetings, I AM AMMORAH

Pleiadian High Priestess on the Pleiadian High Council

Part 46: Dancing to a higher tune of creation

When you have discovered the power of positive thought-power and greater inner fire, you play the game higher.

Together with the celebration of your heart of love you are becoming purposeful creators. You are becoming your stronger self and you are learning to tune in higher to the light of the Cosmic Dances to experience higher frequencies of love.

You must always remember that the Universal Laws always remain the same. Nothing ever changes, and everything always follows cosmic law. When you do things the same way, the result is always the same.

You have discovered this with your hardship and your pain have you not? You have played these same energies over and over again and the result has always been the same.

This is because energy will always flow in the way you direct it, never in the opposite. It is not until you learn to change your rules within your own universal system that your wheel begins to turn towards the love gate.

We have mentioned before there are different dimensions to be discovered within the love dimensions. Some work and some do not work for you. Some will work against your power flows to create your dreams.

You may decide love is love and that all love has equal energy values and you cannot change the power within the love energies.

Herein the mind is greatly challenged, for no energy is equal. It is as if you have a bag of sweets when you give it to your children. They may all belong to the same family but each one has a different flavor or colour.

So it is with energy. They may be classified as 'anger' or 'pain,' or 'love,' but within these exist many categories of energies. Together they create a magnificent soup of energies all mixed collectively, all ready to perform their own dance.

Hence, we ask you to reflect upon your own lessons at this time. Are you ready to dance higher? Are you ready to dance to the higher tune of love? Are you ready to find out how to play the Greater Cosmic Dance?

Love in itself has many dimensions. Some of which you may consider to be high love, but they work against the greater love because they are not 'true' love. Others are based on true love. However, because of the anger and fear you mix in the potion, this love becomes less potent and will work opposite to what you expect.

You are becoming the energy alchemist in this game. Which energy will produce which result? When you add this energy to another, how will the result change?

Imagine if you were standing in a laboratory and you had ten different love energy potions in front of you. How would you name them and define them?

Would you know the difference? Here it is largely up to you to discover.

Many people define love as serving other people. Is this true love, or a need of having love?

We allow you to investigate this issue as this is important for you to discover your motives in your life and your hidden belief patterns.

Many people desire to be needed. They serve others with love to fulfill their own inner emptiness. This is because they do not possess true self-love. Therefore, they are empty within, without vision, without love and without firepower.

They live the illusion that their contentment will be found when they serve others. However, without self-love they will never find deep self fulfilment.

Other people stay in a relationship lacking love because of their children, or perhaps they feel the 'need' to care for their partner and consequently they will not leave the relationship. Many people would call this true dedication and love.

However, they are far from content and inside they feel the emptiness and the loneliness.

Many people feel they 'need' to serve in wars to fight for freedom in your world. Is this true 'love' or is it fear of losing freedom?

Perhaps you call it pride for your country and you call this true love. However, is this true love, or is it fear of not obeying and that somehow you feel the 'need' to listen to the greater authorities, because you fear not being recognized as part of your country, or your 'team.' For many, the fear of not being part of the greater fight runs deep.

Please consider all these points. What do you consider true love to be?

These are considerably deep questions, and deep issues that you as a race face. Individually and collectively you are facing these questions and inner conflicts and you are feeling as if you are dancing a dance, going nowhere.

None of these are true Creator 'Love' energies. None of these give you the strength, fire, wisdom and love to fulfill your dreams and to awaken the creator within you.

A Komo Ha Halima, I AM AMMORAH, Pleiadian Teacher and High Priestess, dwelling with you in eternal peace.

A Komo Ha Halima

Greetings, I AM AMMORAH

Pleiadian High Priestess on the Pleiadian High Council

Part 47: Defining true love

True Love is the greatest and most magical gift you can find in your life. It is fulfilling, loving, flowing, nurturing, forgiving, healing, passionate, complete, warm, strong, inspiring, wise and powerful. It is the gift many have sought for, lifetime after lifetime.

You must learn to find true love within yourselves, for love for life is true love. When you understand the meaning of true love, you feel the passion for life.

Your desire to live and to discover is enormously important to you. You love your freedom and you do the very things you desire for YOU, without any need or hidden motives other than having a deep connection within yourself.

You feel complete within yourself and your masculine and feminine are perfectly balanced and you feel the joy and the love of life.

In the true love you allow your pain to constantly go and you feed from the light, allowing the light to heal you and refresh you to create deeper love for life. You create power and energy within, and you understand how to inspire yourself. Your motivation for all of life is great. You breathe in the love to the world and the world will give you its love back in the mirror of reflections.

In this true Spiritual Dance of Great Love you constantly forgive another and forgive yourself for all the pain and hurt. In this Love Dance you accept yourself as you are. You feel the glow and the warmth of your heart expanding and you feel connected to life and all that is.

In this Love Dance you are playing the dances of the cosmic experiences of life. You are receiving guidance from the Higher Dimensional Plays. You understand your spirit within you is powerful and it plays its tunes incredibly high.

In this Love Dance you understand you are part of something so great and you have a burning desire to understand it more. You expand until you cannot expand anymore and then rest in the light you must.

Then once again, you expand into the deeper growth and deeper self-love. Your connection with all existence becomes greater. You expand in more love and you understand more love and you dance higher in the greatness of all of life.

This is true spiritual love and it is permanent. True love for self and for life always grows. It always inspires and motivates, it heals all and all is healed in the love and the light. All is great and all is enhanced. All is perfect and all is balanced.

The wheel keeps turning and turns towards the gates of love and the love becomes stronger.

The love draws you closer to your Creator, to Source, The Divine One. You feel the Great Love and that Love from the Divine draws you in. Your heart expands and you are delighted to understand that all is an illusion and all is a game and that you are winning, because you understand all is a reflection from within and that reflection is pure love.

A Komo Ha Halima, I AM AMMORAH, Pleiadian High Priestess, guiding you to understand how to walk with greatness.

Spiritual Strengthening
Building the flows of love

Exercise 15: Awaken your heart with love of angels

1. Breathe in and out slowly. Feel your body relax. Feel your feet planted solidly on the earth.

2. Surround yourself with love and light by asking for it. Breathing in the light and breathing out the light.

3. Call a beautiful Angel in front of you and trust it is so. Angels care so much about you.

4. We ask you to feel your heart open to the Love of your Angels and allow them to give you a transmission of love in return.

5. Feel the love enveloping every part of your body. Feel it going through you.

6. With every breath in, you feel yourself growing larger in the Love of your Angels.

7. When you have finished, thank your Angels for being present with you and slowly return to your space of existence.

A Komo Ha Halima

Greetings, I AM AMMORAH

Pleiadian High Priestess on the Pleiadian High Council

Part 48: The ultimate cosmic dance of a human experience

Self-love is power. Self-love is strength. It carries you through difficult times. It carries you through the times of sadness and of self-doubts. Self-love carries you through pain and agonizing moments of life.

Self-love is a treasure for anyone and everyone who finds it. It is a treasure and a true treasure of love for anyone who unearths it.

Self-love, can you define it? Can you explain it? Can you find it? How precious is it to you? How does it relate to finding your creator within?

Your Prime Creator is Pure Love and it exists in dimensions of Greater Love than you can possibly comprehend at this given time. You do not understand Divine Love.

If you felt the intensity of this Divine Love, you would not be able to exist upon your physical plane within your physical body because your physical body could not hold the power of Pure Divine Love.

Divine Love is Pure Power. Divine Love is Pure Force Field. Divine Love desires to expand. The greater its expansion, the more it realizes its desire to expand.

When you as an individual come to know this Great Love, your life becomes completely affected by it. You glow in this Divine Love and you become more love.

Others are then attracted to the love you have because they do not understand why you have this power of attraction. The greater the love force field is within you, the more attractive you become.

Love is attractive and powerful. The majority of people on your plane at this time do not understand Divine Love. They do not understand the grandness of Divine Love, and thus at this stage in your evolution, to find it and to see it in another, is relatively rare.

Self-love in its pure essence is a true treasure that is worth more than all the finest treasures upon your plane, for in this true self-love you discover yourself and the very depth of your being. You begin to dance to a greater, loving dance, which is your dance alone.

The energy body of this person who is connected to these deep levels of love, changes dramatically because of the dance in the Cosmic Spaces.

Their higher abilities become more visible and strong. The words they speak are loving and wise. They will always seek to advance, understanding that all is a lesson and all is constantly reflecting back their love and joy. When challenges come their way, they breathe in the moment and understand they must let it go to move on.

This, for these loving, evolved people, also has drawbacks. They may find others desire a relationship that was not intentionally intended, but because of their attractive, loving energy body pouring healing energies out to others constantly, others feel their warmth and love.

Others around these loving, evolved people may not understand their feelings of attraction. They may have never been subjected to spiritual love and may confuse it with sexual attraction. They may feel their heart opening to the joy and passion of life and the warmth for the first time in this life time.

It can also create envy for those who do not understand how to find it. Many may not understand the rate of this evolution and may be immensely puzzled. This can create the opposite effect to your expectation of a deeper love connection.

Every experience is a reflection of your mirrors within and thus more challenges will be discovered deeper by you.

In this Great Love Dance with Prime Creator, you will find the inner power within you growing strongly. You are finding you are playing musical instruments together within this Divine Dance and you are playing these higher tunes to find a greater beat to play.

You are finding you are in a relationship with creation itself and because of the great love you have found, you are finding a deeper relationship with self.

This is true self-love. It is love for the Divine within you, connecting you back to Divine Source.

When a person is this connected within their hearts to Divinity, this one makes choices purely from the heart. When difficult choices are faced, even though the emotions are still involved, the heart will always guide them to the right path.

The love within the heart of these ones is incredibly strong and this intense love will be as a fire burning within the heart.

This person will dedicate himself (or herself) to their inner fire and their inner self. They will not allow anything to disrupt the greatest dance they have found.

They will live and breathe this inner passion. No other relationship will be as important and come close to this inner passion they have found with creator itself.

This stirs the spirit within more. When the heart is aligned with Divine Creator, the spirit of this person becomes alive with greatness. It creates greater visions to follow as this person becomes more greatly aligned with Higher Will. This person's inner fire is greatly alight with glow and love. Life becomes a greater joy to have.

This person has found the true secret to all of life and that is to be in true alignment with all beauty and love and glory of creation.

When you have mastered this level, there is no need to return to the earth plane anymore. This is the ultimate purpose for a human's evolution, unless he or she desires to return to the earth plane in another incarnation to experience more growth. All is a choice in the Dance of Life. All is grand in the Dance of Life.

This union with the heart and Prime Creator, the two meeting this divine sacred point and allowing expansion to grow at this level, is the ultimate goal for you as a human.

This is the most glorious dance you can have as a person, to dance with the light of eternity, together as one, dancing to the Beat of Divine Love.

You will still receive your challenges, but your strength of your firepower will help overcome those challenges and your strength of your vision will help you to see the greater lessons.

Many around you will not understand this Divine Union. It may seem 'far out,' or 'indescribable,' to most people.

However, for the ones who find this, they invite others to join them as it is a delightful dance for them. For them it is grander than all the delicious food and the finest wine that can be found upon your plane.

It is the ultimate dance of the cosmic dances of the human experience.

A Komo Ha Halima, I AM AMMORAH, Pleiadian High Priestess, we are guiding you to a way of great beauty and love.

A Komo Ha Halima

Greetings, I AM AMMORAH

Pleiadian High Priestess on the Pleiadian High Council

Part 49: The dance of life – a gift from your creators

Your Creators are Star Beings. They borrowed from Source of Prime Creator to create you.

Your Creators are wise and highly intelligent and wanted you to understand all is a perfect gift and all can be created when one is awakened to higher understanding.

They desired you to know that all is possible in the illusion of the energies and that all is not as solid as you may believe it to be.

They desired you to grow with the greater understanding that you are creators yourselves.

When you awaken to the dancing light within you and you dance together with the higher tunes in the universe, working together with the light, filling your hearts with the love of your creators, you can create a beautiful planet together.

Your Creators desired you to understand you have all you need here on your planet. You do not need outside help to help you discover your creator within. All you are required to do is to discover how to be in the light together, to listen to each other, to accept each other and to always stay humble with the knowledge you are great.

However, you are required to learn and to assist others.

You are playing a game in this life-time. The greatest game in this life is to discover the creator within you and to be able to work together as a massive team towards one goal and to join with each other with one heart, unified in purpose.

You as a race have so long been separated. Power struggles are and have been phenomenal among you. Even in small groups you cannot decide how to bring greater love together. You have trouble with this concept of Oneness.

We ask you to leave all your personal feelings behind, to focus on the greater work at hand. Leave all the struggles behind. Leave all your pain behind. Leave all your battles about who is stronger and who is weaker behind.

In the greater scheme of things this has no bearing on anything other than presenting more struggles.

Envy is great in many places on your planet. The attitude of many on your planet is you seem to think that no one is 'supposed' to be greater than you. In many cases if someone has greater talent, many of you try to crush that talent to stop that one rising.

We ask you why? Why do you do this? Can you not see there are masters with you, sent to guide you to greatness, to help you become masters also?

Let go of your pain. Let go of your bitterness. Rejoice in the many gifts and talents of others.

Instead of envying talents and strengths of another, learn from them and also become this great and greater still. Learn to embrace each other. Learn to be friends with everyone and accept each other. All people have many sacred gifts to share.

To stand in the power of your creator-self, you must learn to become more love. It is learning how to step into that and to join the dance of the Greater Love in the Cosmic Dances of Love, for all is one and all is considered as perfect.

This is your greatest challenge to change your earth plane. You must learn to dance together to the same beat. You must learn to rejoice with each other. You must learn to accept each other as one and as great and to greet each other with your heart of love.

When you do this, you will grow within your lives.

On our plane, on the Pleiadian Realms, we have different evolution growths.

We, in the Great Light, have evolved far beyond the pain and the trouble you know well on your plane. We have distanced ourselves from the pettiness because we understand that to dance with our Creators in light and to dance with the Great Light of our Prime Creator we must step into the Great Oneness.

We have worked hard and continue to work hard at this. We have advanced to such a high spiritual level we are able to appreciate the gifts of our brothers and sisters and to grow strongly into their gifts.

We can take on the greater gifts our brothers and sisters have and rejoice in them. We do not have jealousy among us. We understand the disease of envy and jealousy. We only shine in our light and we encourage our brothers and sisters to shine in their light also, to give glory to the Grand Creator and to all things that are Divine.

We understand the Great Dance of the Universal Flow. We understand the Great Oneness. We understand the Connection of the Great One and that all is One and we are not separate from each other. We accept this beauty and greatness within ourselves.

We have a deep self-love and self-respect for ourselves. We honor the greatness within us.

You would do well to take on these great lessons as you would see the incredible growth happening within you.

We understand we can learn from each other. When one of our brothers or sisters outshines another and masters a gift, we never belittle them or envy their gifts.

Instead we stand in their gift. We stand in their energy and ask the Great Spirit to endow us with the same gifts of Spirit.

We rejoice in these gifts because these Sacred Gifts are sent to our Pleiadian Realms to help us step up greater in our evolution.

You have much to learn from these lessons, for many of you do the opposite.

We advise you to change as a race. Embrace each other. See your gifts as the gifts of Holy Spirit. See these gifts as Sacred. They are deeply Sacred.

Rejoice and embrace each other. Learn to be at one with each other.

A Komo Ha Halima, we are a group of Light Healers and Light Shiners, shining the way before you to share the love within you, to share the love with each other, dancing the Dance of Light together.

A Komo Ha Halima

Greetings, I AM AMMORAH

Pleiadian High Priestess on the Pleiadian High Council

Part 50: Awakening your sacred creator flow

Many of your people on your earth plane have turned off their sacred creator. They have become numb to her Sacredness. They have become numb to their feelings and as a result, they cannot express their 'self' any longer.

The sacred creator, when she is freed, will fulfill you, will empower you, will work with you to create your desires and will help you to become free. She is playful, highly intuitive and highly sexual.

When you awaken your Sacred Goddess, you become stronger within. Your heart opens to the dance of light which is Sacred and ancient. This is your dance and it is the dance that has always been yours to have.

As a race, you have been greatly hurt with your sexuality. You have become lost with its sacred meaning. You do not understand how powerful your sexuality is. Many of you have come to fear it. With many, it has caused confusion and pain. You have learned to set boundaries and a great number of you do not desire to cross these boundaries that you believe are right.

You sexually feel (here I will talk generally) in pain, as if you cannot discover what is yours to have, as if it is perhaps not to be mentioned. It may be embarrassing to discuss. It may be considered 'dirty.'

To others, they have lost the sacredness of sexuality. They will talk about sexuality flamboyantly, not caring about the feelings of others. They become lustful, as if without caring for others and self.

Many people on your plane are incredibly confused in the sea of sexuality. They search for many partners, always looking for that special one who can give them ecstasy and who are willing to play their rules.

However, this is far from the Sacred Sexuality you were created with. Divine Sexuality is powerful, grand and almighty.

Can you not see this is a gift from your Creators to not only use it for procreation, but also to co-create a beautiful harmony together and to sing the songs of your Creators in the Light?

It is a sacred gift for you, given to you to sing to a higher tune of awakening. When you find the Sacred Goddess within you, you will set yourselves free from all these beliefs that have limited you and pained you for so long.

We, as Pleiadians in the light are highly playful when it comes to our sexuality. We are serious with our commitments. We do not have multiple partners and we keep faithful to ourselves.

When we have intimacy, we have it to create a greater harmony within ourselves. We learn to discover ourselves more. We create greater portals of love within ourselves. We create love that is complete on our plane. We create a greater loving space for our partners and to create a greater creation field for ourselves.

Our play is always about expansion and development. We always create. We always seek expansion.

When we have intimacy with a partner we care deeply about, we bond deeply. Not only for this lifetime, but we remember our soul contract before we came to our Pleiadian Realms and we awaken to our deeper selves. We awaken to a deeper part within us. We realize how important our lives are and what our greater mission is.

This is what many beings of the darkness do not want you to understand. This is why 'sexual intimacy,' has always been kept dull, restricted and quiet on your plane. This is why many of the dark ones put fear into people's minds about their sexuality rather than true enjoyment and awakening.

Sexual freedom brings you greater enlightenment and creates a deeper sacred space within you to heal and to learn in.

In this lesson, we endeavor to help you understand how important you are as a race and how important you are to yourself.

Your sexual restriction has created a huge halt to your personal spiritual development. It creates confusion on your plane. It has caused rebellion and fear. It has helped to cause many murders and pain.

Sexual attraction can either be misused or used for healing purposes. It can be used for 'dark' purposes and for 'light' purposes.

Like all things in your life, everything upon your plane, all decisions, all choices are up to you. You can stay the way you are, or you can learn to free yourselves.

We are your tutors and we are guiding you to your greater freedom, to your creator within you, to set you free.

We ask you; are you ready to discover yourselves on a deeper, intimate level?

A Komo Ha Halima, I AM AMMORAH, Pleiadian High Priestess, we are here to share with you our love and our guidance.

The sacred dance together

In your Sacred Dance,

together,

you join together,

in a celebration of love,

to discover together,

to open together,

to deeper awareness,

to deeper discovery,

of love and harmony,

to deeper tunes within you,

together with the stars,

celebrating,

as One in great love harmony.

A Komo Ha Halima

Greetings, I AM AMMORAH

Pleiadian High Priestess on the Pleiadian High Council

Part 51: You are sacred beings of creation

Before you learn how to free your sacred sexuality, to feel and desire your internal Sacred Goddess and to celebrate your intimate union, you must learn about why you are sexual beings.

Sexuality is important. It is sacred. It goes beyond the desire and the need for children.

If your Creators had not created you with a Sacred Sexuality and if the reason for this intimacy was only to have children, they would not have created you as beautiful as you are.

You are beautiful beings. You are exquisitely made. You are highly playful and highly creative.

The greater your sexual charge is in the highest most healing sacred ways, the greater the creator within you is able to show. Your sexuality and your inner fire are both connected within you on deep sacred levels.

Your sacred sexuality is held in great respect in the Universe. Your Creators do not consider your sexuality as 'dirty,' or 'wrong,' in any way. They consider it as 'holy,' when it is used for healing purposes.

You have forgotten, by and large, to understand its 'Holiness.' You have believed it to be otherwise. You do not celebrate the union of your coming together as you originally were created to do. You do not understand that you can discover your true selves and the Universe together and to create a union, not only with your physical selves but with deep energetic bonds of love.

Bonding energetically is a far greater experience, with greater enjoyment and excitement when the dance of the energy level and the physical level come together in a sacred union.

This creates a deep connection between self and your inner creator. The connection and the bond between your loved one and yourself deepens. This is the Sacred Dance of Sexual Bonding.

Sexual intimacy on the physical level alone is not healing for you. It is not deeply fulfilling. We say it does the opposite. We say it is harmful and deeply empty.

Many of you are finding this on your plane. Many women and men are deeply sexually unfulfilled. Many of you do not understand why you feel unhappy when you do not receive this deep intimacy. You do not understand what it is you are searching for and thus you are left without answers, as if a huge gap is waiting to be filled.

We desire to help you understand what it is you are searching for and then to help you to find it.

You are searching for a deeper connection within yourselves. This deep connection within, when you can celebrate it together with a loved one, becomes a deep union between the two of you.

People on your plane are not taught this great celebration of a holy intimate relationship. You have 'sexual education,' on your plane and you hear about how not to contract a disease or avoid having babies.

To understand the 'Sacred Sexuality Dance,' is priceless.

Sexual intimacy is to have a sacred union with self on deeper levels of dance. It is to become aware you carry both male and female energy and you create a union within self to bring these two aspects of self together, into a Sacred Bond of Love.

The masculine and the feminine parts are both equally important in the flow of your life. When these two are in perfect harmony together, your life becomes magnificent. Each part has a role to play and each keeps the other happy.

It is as if you create a divine marriage between the Sacred Masculine and the Sacred Feminine within you. You create the power and the love. You create the strength and the passion.

When a person has truly found the harmony between these two parts within themselves, their Sacred Goddess becomes incredibly powerful. The Sacred Goddess is fully aware of her desires. She will create ways of love within herself and she will turn all her attention to further awareness of how to create deeper bonds of love within herself.

When you find this inner power, you have awoken your Sacred Creator. The result for you is incredibly wonderful. You will enjoy ecstasy on great levels. This is your reward, for she rewards you well.

You are discovering these two aspects of yourself, regardless of your male or female identity at this time. You are discovering the creator and the creator within you and the two, when they come in union, will bring you enlightenment and awakening. They bring you into a sacred truth of who you truly are. They will bring you into a sacred beauty and a sacred light.

When you become aware of this, you begin to understand why many of you feel unfulfilled in a sexual relationship. You may think it is the other that 'should' be more giving, or 'pleasing.' However, this play is not about the other. This play is about finding the sacred union within. This is what you are truly searching for.

When you discover the magnificent relationship between your masculine and feminine, sacred dimensions open within you and you open to deeper love.

The people of the old knew the secrets well. They often made 'love' with their partners together to create one large portal of light for them to grow in together. This is how many of the old grew spiritually together rapidly and their greater gifts began to shine.

We as Pleiadians are also playful together, though we hold our sacred partners as sacred and we choose one partner. We commit to one partner with a deep, mutual sacred dance of love for growth, love, expansion within ourselves and within each other.

This is because that special partner in our lives has the ability to open us to a deeper self. Our partners also have a special union within themselves and because they have created this space of growth they are able to help their partner open up to deeper love and growth.

We dance the Sacred Dance together.

This is how sacred our sexuality is to us. You do not yet understand how sacred it is. We wonder if you realize how damaging it is for you to have multiple partners. Not only because of diseases you may contract, or relationship issues, but because you are damaging yourselves on deeper sacred, spiritual levels.

When you hold your sexuality sacred, you begin to open your higher gifts more easily and it becomes a deeply fulfilling and sacred play.

When you choose to have 'one night' sleepovers with anyone who sees you at that time, you become more lost, more lonely and you create more fear in life. You become more insecure of who you are and you become greatly unbalanced.

Depression is very likely and you will have trouble settling down because of your habit of moving from one partner to another. You will keep looking for that 'special' one, but you will not be able to find that one because you do not understand that to find that 'special' one, you must find that 'special' union within yourselves first.

Each time you create a 'sexual play' with a partner, you are not only merging physically, but you are also taking on the energetic blueprint of the other, creating a greater soup for you to feel in, to discover in, to become confused in. You are taking on their belief systems, their challenges, their fears and their thought patterns.

Sexual intimacy is far greater than you realize.

Therefore, when you have Sacred Sexuality and you merge with a loving partner who you are compatible with, you not only join them emotionally and physically, but you also merge on deep spiritual planes.

You feel the love you have for your partner and you open your heart to the love of self, to your deep union within self and then you open to the dimensions of love together, creating greater harmony to play in.

You deepen the relationship within yourself and you are finding your Sacred Goddess within and this opens your sacred fire and passion.

You are in that moment your own creators. You are creating your play of light. You are discovering the beauty of yourselves and you are able to create greatness and sacred play together. Your strengths increase because you are becoming energetically stronger in the love for yourselves and for each other.

How then do you work towards this incredible sexual play? How do you learn to do this? We will teach you and guide you in the following lesson.

A Komo Ha Halima, I AM AMMORAH, Pleiadian High Priestess, guiding you to greater fulfillment and deeper love connections.

A Komo Ha Halima

Greetings, I AM AMMORAH

Pleiadian High Priestess on the Pleiadian High Council

Part 52: Becoming sacred dancers

To feel the love for all of life, to dance to the greatness, to feel the Sacred Goddess dancing with you, to play in the greater Cosmic Dance, means to understand you are sacred and you are completely accepted and loved by Divine Beings.

There does not exist; 'You should do this or you should not do that,' for sexual play is sacred in the eyes of your Creators and your Prime Creator. There is nothing more beautiful to your Creators than learning to understand who you are on this deep sexual level.

You were created to do this. You were created in such a way, that if you knew how to play this game right, you would open portals of love within self and then deeper understanding of self would follow.

To receive this, your growth as spiritual beings need to be fully grounded first.

You are a spiritual being. A being who needs spiritual nourishment. Sexual play, in these highest ways, is spiritually nourishing. When you receive this, you feel deeply content and fulfilled. You become greatly excited and your energy levels rise. Thus, you become more attractive and greatly sexual beings.

You gain a greater awareness of what you do desire and what you do not desire. Your throat chakra becomes healed because you are opening your sexuality and your throat chakra is expressing your sexuality in a most beautiful and magnificent way.

You become an expression of love.

You also must learn to love yourselves and to understand you are beings of love. You must learn to understand you were created in a highly playful energy and to feel highly sexual is part of your gift. To be able to express it is an incredible gift of love, for you and for your partner.

To create a deeper union with self is a sacred healing process of total forgiveness for having been hurt in the past and to come to a full acceptance of who you are.

When you learn to forgive your past partners and the people who have hurt you in this deep intimate way, you will have the freedom to discover greater depth of who you truly are.

We ask you to request for guidance on learning how to forgive, for you are as individuals very important in the eyes of Spirit, your Creators and Prime Creator.

You must understand that forgiveness is about allowing self to become free, to discover your Sacred Goddess herself.

Holding on to pain is harmful and punishing. Let it go and feel the love returning to you.

To let go of your pain, means to go to a deep place within your heart, to accept all that has happened. It means you are ready to embrace, to allow you to be in a deep sacred place of love.

To release the past and embrace who you are, imagine for a moment you are standing in a dense forest. This forest is a sacred ancient forest of love and magic.

This forest has the ability to take your past pain away, to allow you to flow with life deeper into the Sacred Love Dance.

For a moment, bring to your mind some of the pain that has deeply troubled you and has stopped you from moving forward into your Sacred Loving Dance.

Allow that to come to your mind and say firmly, 'I am now willing to release it with love and to forgive it. It has taught me well and it has gifted me with strengths. I am willing to let the pain go.'

See it being taken away by the forest, deep within the forest. It will be taken care off and healed to allow you to grow into the love and to dance a Greater Love Dance with your sacred loving hearts, to feel the union and love grow with great fulfilment and great joy.

Upon releasing your pain and allowing your pain to be forgiven, you are now learning to dance the Sacred Loving Dance with the loving energies. You are being freed from your pain and burdens.

You must keep repeating these same processes as often as you need to and allow yourself to go to the very depth of your sacred loving heart to discover the pain, to discover obstacles you have created.

To have a sacred union with a special person in your life means to connect deep with each other and to have a deep respect for each other. Each partner has different needs, and each must be free to speak about these needs and be listened to.

Open communication is vital in the dance of Sacred Sexuality.

You have sacred contracts with people around you as you are working in a cosmic relationship with cosmic dances.

You are there to support each other, learn from each other and dance the higher light with others. You are there to help each other grow and to learn sacred love from each other.

You have chosen your partners who would dance the greater spiritual dance with you, that special dance, the Sacred Dance you would do together when you awakened. We ask you, have you found your partner yet or have you not awoken to that partner yet?

This Sacred Dance is to awaken the Sacred Goddess within you, to awaken the creator energy within you. Creator energy is life giving. A force that is highly playful and highly sexual. It is a dance between the dances into the beauty of who you are.

Many people on your earth plane have difficulty going to this deep, sacred space because of beliefs, traditions and the ways of having been brought up in your society.

We, your Tutors of the Pleiadian Realms of Light, have already discussed with you this is where you will find your higher freedom.

To be able to dance with a loved one in this High Creation Dance will allow you to become free on many levels to reach Sacred Levels of Greatness.

To learn to trust in a loving relationship is important and it is sacred.

When we, as Pleiadian light beings, have sacred relationships, we trust each other. We learn to trust each other by connecting deep within ourselves and within each other.

To connect within the eyes is connecting to a deep space of love. To connect within the hearts, is to communicate deeper and to create a deep, sacred space for learning to dwell in love with each other.

Learn to listen to each other. Learn to listen to each other's desires when it comes to this sacred space. Learn to be open and learn to please each other by dancing this sacred dance within.

Feel free, playful, trusting the other and learn to dance in the light. Open to each other and be in sacred communication.

To free the Goddess inside of you is a deep place to reach. It is sacred, precious and deeply spiritual as you are reaching into the life-force energy with which you were created.

This sacred fire energy is an intense passionate energy. When you reach into this energy, your health becomes stronger, you become greatly empowered. These vital life-force energies help you to understand the creator within you and your dreams become greater as a result.

Your fire energies will help you with manifesting your sacred purpose of why you are on your earth plane at this time.

It is when you dance with these Sacred Energies, your lives become stronger and you will feel the power within you grow.

We wish to help you with a healing to help you find your Sacred Goddess within.

As you do these exercises, be assured we are holding the space for your growth and we are healing your frequencies to help you discover your greater self.

A Komo Ha Halima, I AM AMMORAH, Pleiadian High Priestess, we are here to help you become free from pain.

Spiritual Strengthening
Building the flows of love

Exercise 16: Release your pain

1. Surround yourself in the greatness of the love of the Great Light of the universe. Call in your Angels as they care for you and love you. They know you very well and understand how you are feeling. They understand your hurt and pain and the great desire within you to heal.

2. We ask you to call in four Pleiadians in the light. One will be with you standing on your right hand side, one on your left hand side, one in front of you and one behind you.

3. We will create a field of light around you, holding you in a sacred space of love and healing to help you discover your passion for life, to discover your love and to help you find your Sacred Goddess.

4. Breathe in the energies as we are transmitting the correct energies to you, to hold you in this space of love.

5. We are healing your chakra gateways at this time and your deeper layers within you to give you the space and the room to grow in.

6. Go deeper within your heart with an understanding we are fully supporting you.

7. Bring in a double self, to allow you to relate and express your desires and pain.

8. Speak about your pain. Your double self will listen as you express your pains, desires and thoughts.

9. Free yourself from your pain. Say: 'I allow myself to be freed from my pain, I forgive myself and all others for the pain they have caused me and I have caused myself. I release it now in the light to become healed.'

10. Visualize yourself standing in front of a river. The current is strong and it will carry your old pain and baggage away to a grand healing place.

11. A bag is beside you now. Within it, place all the pain and everything you desire to release, whether it is past relationships, past beliefs, past situations. After placing your pain in the bag, throw it in the river and see it being carried away.

12. We ask you to witness the bag being carried down the stream.

13. Very slowly come back to your plane, breathing in and out deeply, thanking all who supported you and open your eyes.

14. Feel refreshed and relieved.

15. Well done, you have done much to free yourself. You are ready to climb to a new level of dance.

A Komo Ha Halima

Greetings, I AM AMMORAH

Pleiadian High Priestess on the Pleiadian High Council

Part 53: Creating a sacred space of growth

Your Sacred Goddess will create an incredibly powerful energy for you. Your Sacred Goddess will help you to feel great passion because you are learning to have a relationship with self. This self-relationship is sacred, creating a greater space of healing for you.

When you have achieved this grand union of the sacred space of the masculine and the feminine energy, your inner fire discovers the creator you are within.

To reach this deeper level takes great healing. Please understand, we as your Pleiadian healers of light are guiding you through processes to help you to learn this sacred space of reaching your creator abilities within.

When you grow to these deep levels, you will desire to create a sacred space of growth within you. This space of growth is important to feel your love for who you are, to understand your passion, your desires and to grow in the enormous light you are creating.

We ask you to build your light every day. We will give you an exercise with your Pleiadian light healers at the end of this chapter on how to build that light and to build your strength and your love.

When you dance these higher cosmic dances, your desire to join the Great Cosmic Dance of Love with Beings of Love expands. They desire to help you develop these greater strengths, to allow you to flow with love, abundance, happiness, wisdom, pride, courage, strength, power, happiness, success and health.

You as a race have become distanced from your sacred heart. You, as a whole, have forgotten about the sacredness of your creation and have lost your precious pride and harmony.

When you begin to awaken your inner creator, you will long to dance in this sacred union of these deeper sacred spaces within your heart.

It is then your energy frequency and your whole understanding of life begins to take on powerful changes.

You will choose to look upwards and inwards instead of outside of yourself. You awaken to what is light and what are shadows of the light. Your decisions will be based on deeper wisdom, instead of what people may believe or what people say.

Peer pressure has been an enormous task for you to cope with in your society. You have listened to others and conformed to the standards of others and have relied too much on opinions of others. You believe each other's ideas; especially those of your teachers.

We as Pleiadians in the light understand these belief systems very well. We understand why you feel the need to do this. This is because you have lost sacred connection with your Sacred Self and you have distanced self from Source. You have forgotten your inner power, strength and wisdom.

It is as if you are walking around trying to find the switch to turn your light on to find your treasures in your heart. You keep looking outside of self to find the switch, but you are unable to find it. It is as if you grope in the darkness to try and find the light.

On the way to finding the light you may have trouble seeing, because many of you are afraid to look into the light. You are afraid because you have a deep knowing it will awaken you from your sleepy dream state.

The sleepy state is where you find your greatest comfort before you awaken.

Once you awaken you become aware of your inner self and you will feel the need to journey into the depths of your heart.

Gone are the times when you allowed yourself to be numb to life. Now you are learning to understand the truth of the light. You are discovering your truth.

Once you surrender to the light, life becomes easier.

Once you awaken you will see the ones who are still asleep. You will see the ones who are searching to find the switch to the light but have not yet found it.

You will feel for them. You will try and reach out to them. You will understand that they too need to be willing to find the light in their hearts to discover truth for themselves before they find the 'switch.'

It is only then that they will yearn to find the sacred space of Divine Love in their hearts and their connection to the Great Light, which has always been there.

To find the light is not easy. You have been taught to judge it and not trust it.

It is not always easy to find the Great Light because in general you have become confused and cannot define light from darkness anymore.

To truly find the light switch you must reach within your heart and allow guidance to come through. It is the only way to find this switch.

Light is magnificent. It is power. It is love. It is life-force. It is creation. It is knowledge. It is wisdom. It is might. It is pride. It is filled with energy to heal. It is free. It is truth. It is freeing for the people who find it. It is precious. It is available to anyone who desires it.

To switch the light on you must learn to create a sacred space to be in the light of your soul, to be in the light of your power.

We would like to help you with this. When you do this following exercise regularly greater benefits will come your way and greater understanding becomes yours to have.

A Komo Ha Halima, I AM AMMORAH, Pleiadian High Priestess. We as your Pleiadian Light Healers are here to guide you to Greater Light and Divine Wisdom.

Spiritual Strengthening
Building the flows of love

Exercise 17: Build your power

1. Begin by relaxing for a while. Simply breathe in and out, slowly relaxing your body.

2. Surround yourself in magnificent light and call in your Angels in the light to help you to become more light.

3. Ask for your Pleiadian healers in the light. Four will help you with transmissions of light. One will be standing on your right, one on your left, one behind you and one in front of you.

4. Breathe in the love they are transmitting to you now. We are holding the frequencies for your healing and we are setting the space for your magnificent wisdom to open.

5. We would like you to visualize an incredible sun up above you. You feel drawn to that sun and you are feeling the sun drawing closer to you.

6. This sun is the sun of your light of your soul. It has high frequencies and when you are with this light, you become more beautiful and your light beautifies. You feel the power of who you are and your gifts increase when you sit in this sun.

7. You may visualize yourself sitting in this sun. This sun is not your literal sun and it will not burn you. It is a soft sun, a powerful spiritual sun. The light will strengthen your life and create a greater force within you.

8. Breathing in and out, trusting we are holding the space for your

sacred healing. You are creating your own space for your sacred healing and you are becoming stronger and more empowered. Your love for life will grow each time you create this space for your healing and your visions will become greater. You will grow with deeper love for who you are.

9. Slowly breathe in and out and release yourself from your sacred space.

Well done on creating your sacred space.

A Komo Ha Halima

Greetings, I AM AMMORAH

Pleiadian High Priestess on the Pleiadian High Council

Part 54: Searching for your wisdom

In your search to finding your creator within, your desire to learn deeper energy play and to learn how to use your energy to create larger dances of flow will increase.

The greater the flow and love within you, the greater your awareness grows, the greater your desire will become to nourish who you are.

As you read these pages and work with us, your whole energy game changes. You are learning to understand how to play with higher energies. As a result, your power to create abundance and love increases.

As you grow up in your society you are not taught about your energy force. You are not equipped to learn how to handle yourselves energetically.

Disease occurs not only on the physical, mental and emotional layers but also on deeper energetic layers. To learn how to stay strong on the energetic layers, it is necessary to understand your multidimensional play.

When you do not focus upon your multidimensional play, you create issues in life when you do not understand these deeper layers.

Your energy layers and your greater self-layers are more important to you than you realize. They live on higher dimensions than your physical layer and they keep evolving. They keep growing. They keep expanding.

Hence, the term 'unlimited,' because the greater the expansion within these higher layers become, the greater your evolution becomes.

These layers live in higher dimensions and create dances of their own. We will teach you this in the future as the depth of your dance will become greater and then it will become necessary to open you to that higher information.

Learn one dance step at a time. The beat is becoming faster and greater. It has become more exciting for us also as dancers to watch you grow and take on higher knowledge and greater steps of wisdom. You are certainly learning fast in these times of acceleration.

We wish to say to you at this time, well done for coming to the Cosmic Dance. You are magnificent playful beings and we wish to join you now as you learn more about energy play and how you can bring more of your life-force energies towards you, to bring a life you truly desire.

Your physical body is only a very small part of you. It is the part you relate to each day. It is the part you play your dance with on the physical plane. It is the part you associate with in your life.

The other parts of your higher energy levels are magnificent and always have been with you. They grow with you, expand with you, love you, understand your deeper purpose records all your thoughts and all your life times. They hold your deeper layers of your DNA and a perfect pattern of your perfect self. Constantly they keep creating your life.

Yes, it constantly creates your life. Your higher levels are constantly creating, depending on how you play your universal laws within your own universe. You are creating these laws and you are constantly programming your life.

You are programmers of yourself, of your own software. When you are not aware of it you do not realize it, and this is when you are oblivious to the positives and negatives of this game. It is as if you were in a large chess game without understanding how to make the next move.

As you can see from this example, without grasping the rules to win the game of chess it would be called 'luck,' in your society.

We say luck does not exist.

Everything is constantly in movement and constantly being created. Life-force energy can become stronger or weaker, depending on how you play the energy game and depending on how you dance your tune.

You can create your life with all the frequencies you desire because you are surrounded by frequencies.

Remembering your sacred eye (your inner eye), is a powerful portal. All your visions and thoughts become a part of your play depending on your focus and depending on your desires at the time of your creation.

When you understand how to play this dance, you are able to find the creator within you. The beauty of this dance is it has some rules to live by. It has guidelines and they will never change.

However, when you do not understand these guidelines you will not know how to adhere to them and thus you will lose the rhythm and you will dance to the beat of disharmony in your life.

We ask you to look within your life and feel the truth of this. How has your life been affected by disharmony? Perhaps if you had known how to dance to the tune of the higher beat, much of your pain could have been avoided.

Here we ask you to always be ready to let go of your past pain and to forgive it, because otherwise you cannot play to the higher beat.

When you hold on to past pain, you create the same frequencies within the cloud of space to repeat the same dance again in the future. This is because you are good at programming your personal universe to act out what you believe will happen.

A Komo Ha Halima, we are your Healers of Light and we are assisting you to a way of higher love consciousness.

Guidelines to dance the dance of energy power faster and higher:

💜 One is encouraged to always forgive the past, people and situations in life. One is encouraged to always truly release it and let it go.

💜 One is encouraged to always express love and light within their lives and let all pain go. This includes the pain of other people who suffer.

💜 One is encouraged always to sit in the light of the Great Love to release the pain and to receive greatness and power, to find wisdom within.

💜 One is encouraged to always feel the sacred space within for stronger guidance and greater healing.

💜 One is encouraged to always express high wisdom in their lives and embrace the truth of who they truly are. They will then embrace the truth of others and see each other as sacred beings.

♥ One is encouraged to always be ready to listen to self and to go within to find their greater desires. This will build the greatness of love and build the greater visions in life.

♥ One is encouraged to always be actively seeking greater ways of evolution for then greater firepower will come and the power of the manifestations of desires and healings will become stronger.

A Komo Ha Halima

Greetings, I AM AMMORAH

Pleiadian High Priestess on the Pleiadian High Council

Part 55: Discovering the importance of forgiveness

Master Teacher Jesus always taught about the important practice of forgiving. He understood the secret to receiving greater strength.

In his days, people held a lot of hate for each other and they constantly fought and bickered about who was the greatest and who did the worst of things.

Jesus stepped into their center and said to them, 'Brothers, learn to embrace each other. You are here to shine and learn to be kind to each other. Can you not see that you are all important? Can you not see you are here to teach each other how to accept one another?

'Learn to forgive each other. Learn to let it go. Shake hands. Let it go. Learn to be at peace with each other. Learn to understand you are both from light. Go now and be at peace.'

He understood the pain anger causes and how to heal it.

You are all magnificent beings. You have so much love to grow with. Yet, you do not how to look after your love. You do not understand your inner beauty.

You keep giving all your power away with your fear, your anger and your hurt. You keep scattering your energies into other directions, instead of bringing them to yourself to use with your power manifestations. You are deadening your feelings when you are in pain. You are still living in the past when you are in the hurt.

Many people on your plane do not understand they are dancing to the tune of pain and anger. This beat is very, very heavy and with each step they become more tired, more 'drained.' Your energy constantly escapes to other directions and therefore you lose strength for your happiness and health in your own lives.

Your frequencies then become confused. They follow your command as you are the commander of your own universal system within you. When your frequencies are confused, they do not relate to the Greater Dance. Your dance is out of order, out of balance, out of tune and certainly will not bring greatness to life.

In order to awaken your creator within, it is essential to align your energy forces with harmony, love, strength and greatness.

When you are scattered with pain, these frequencies are misaligned and hence your pain and confusion increases. You will feel as if your purpose has drifted to the far distance and depression and sadness results from unbalanced frequencies.

Many of you visit your medical professionals when you feel 'unbalanced,' and 'unable to cope.' They prescribe you with drugs. Your energy body, because it responds to everything on your physical level, begins to react to these drugs and more unbalance occurs within your energy body.

Thus, in order to break the true cycle of pain, it is important to understand you on the deeper levels.

As we stated before, you are a multidimensional being. There are many dimensions which you dwell in. Your higher dimensions live in greater dimensions of love; thus, you are in 'reality', surrounded in love and light.

However, because of painful frequencies of pain, hurt and anger, you cannot reach these higher dimensions of your light body because of interference of your pain.

If you learned to clear yourselves, you would be able to reach these higher dimensions and experience the greater love and light.

Please understand the beauty of you. Consider all these points. Perhaps draw a diagram of what we as Pleiadian healers in the light have taught you here. You are a magnificent, beautiful being of light.

The way to clear these frequencies to reach higher frequencies and to align yourself to the greater force within you to awaken the creator within you, is to learn to forgive and release all your pain, fear and anger.

Pain, fear and anger carry a denser energy and stop your greatness coming through. The denser energies will attract more of the same old frequencies of pain for you to experience the same dance, until you begin to change the beat.

This is why, to stop the broken record in your life repeating over and over with the same frequencies of your own creations, you must learn to change the frequency of your story.

Forgiveness is about freeing you, to allow love to come through and help you dance to a love dance of life.

Your anger, pain and unhappiness create a cage around you. In this cage you feel locked in. At times you may feel claustrophobic and you may have trouble breathing.

You create your own cage with your dance of life and your beat. Your inner beliefs reflect back your fears and your pain.

In this cage, you may be blaming others for creating the pain. Your anger runs deep. The greater your pain, the greater the prison you have created for yourself.

When you begin to understand the power of forgiveness, the cage lifts and you are able to walk more with freedom. Your fear becomes less because you become more trusting. You stop being angry with your world because you begin to understand the great Oneness and that you are part of the Oneness. You understand everyone in your world is playing a part in your theatre that you have created in your own universal laws of existence.

You are setting yourselves free.

Can you understand from this illustration the power of freedom from anger, pain and fear?

We have given to you the following exercise to help you with forgiveness. We ask you to do this regularly when you feel it is necessary to let go of your pain.

The person you will call in works on higher levels. This person will not become angry with you and will not argue with you. You are free to speak.

The more you play the tune of forgiveness, the greater the freedom becomes. Always be in the loving, always be in the forgiving and allow all else to be released. This will set you free to create higher creations of beauty and love in your life.

A Komo Ha Halima, I AM AMMORAH, Pleiadian High Priestess, guiding you to a way of greatness and freedom.

Spiritual Strengthening
Building the flows of love

Exercise 18: Deep journey of forgiveness

1.   Relax your body. Surround yourself with light, Divine Love and your Angels who will fully support you with your journey of growth and love. Deeply relax, breathing in and out. Slowly inhaling and slowly exhaling.

2.   Call in your Pleiadian healing guides in the light. Two will be on either side of you. One will be behind you and one in front of you.

3.   You are now going to relax deeper as we are placing frequencies of love into you stronger.

4.   We ask you to visualize a beautiful garden. This garden is magnificent with many varieties of flowers and plants. All these are calming for you. You are relaxing deeper.

5.   You are seeing a park bench and you are invited to sit on the park bench.

6.   You are surrounded by your Angels and your Healing Team of Pleiadians.

7.   We ask you to bring in a person who hurt you very much in your life. We ask you to express your pain and hurt towards this person and release it with love.

8.   Say: 'I forgive you for all the pain you have caused me. I also forgive myself for the pain I have caused myself. Thank you for sharing your gifts with me. I have learned much. I let you go

now. Peace be with you, as peace is with me.'

9.   Then see this person leave.

10.   Slowly bring yourself back through the breath to your dimension
      at this time.

Well done on allowing your anger to be released.

A Komo Ha Halima

Greetings, I AM AMMORAH

Pleiadian High Priestess on the Pleiadian High Council

Part 56: Your eternal existence

Congratulations for coming to this part. You have learned much with us and we ask you to read slowly through these pages, to help you to see your world differently and help you to understand the energy plays upon your plane and within your lives, to help you discover your creator power within.

Already you have discovered very much about the energy plays and how they change. They can enhance your life or cause you misery. All is a reflection of the plays you hold within.

When you believe in love and greatness and you play in these higher fields of magic, your reflection will allow you to experience love. Thus, it is always important to see what needs to be released. Discover where your pain is held and always be in the forgiving and the releasing.

As we continue on our journey together through these pages, you will explore yourself more energetically.

Again, we will say to you this. You are a magnificent creation and your Creators are wise beings. You hold magical gifts within you that are still waiting to be discovered.

Together, you will begin to heal your pain from your past and learn to bring in love and peace.

You have discovered the power of forgiveness. It is important to be in the forgiveness also for your world. Constantly be in the forgiving. Let all the pain go from you, to allow you not to be affected by pain.

Pain will always weaken you. Love and joy will always strengthen you. These are the plays of energies and these plays are important for the ones who desire to play higher in the Cosmic Energies of Love.

A small part of you is physical. Your physical body is important to help you discover your physical plane, your emotions, your relationships with others, your spirituality and your connection to life.

You have already discovered your spirit within and how important it is to allow more of your spirit to join you in your physical 'reality' of life to experience greater love.

We have already taught you about your higher layers around you. These higher layers expand and grow. Eternally they dance in the light you are. They are layers of incredible intelligence and they record everything you experience in all your lifetimes.

They hold records of your illnesses in all your lifetimes. They hold records of all your loves in all your lifetimes also.

DNA blueprints on higher energy levels are perfect and they are waiting for the time to match your physical DNA to create pure love and harmony within your existence.

These layers around you are alive. They are more alive than you on the physical level. They are constantly in communication with higher levels and higher Source of Light.

Without these higher layers your life would not exist. There are many layers of energy and each has a vital role to play in your evolution.

These higher layers are eternally with you and help you remember who you are on the soul level when you are ready to understand.

Thus, the greater the person evolves, the greater the knowledge of your spiritual self becomes as these layers sing with you in greater harmony. This is the greatest song in your evolution, to be able to understand these Divine Layers and how you are connected to the star systems, to all your past and to your future. You are eternal energy, dancing with other energy, magnificent in every way.

A Komo Ha Halima, I AM AMMORAH, Pleiadian High Priestess, guiding you to greatness.

A Komo Ha Halima

Greetings, I AM AMMORAH

Pleiadian High Priestess on the Pleiadian High Council

Part 57: Learning about your energy grid for your greater health

We are here as a group of Pleiadian healers in the light, helping you to find greatness, to help you to find your strength and inner power to create the life you desire.

You have discovered much throughout these pages and you have gained much wisdom.

Already you are dancing to a higher tune in the universe because your awareness is expanding.

Finding your inner strength is important in your world. Losing your strength is easy for you to do. You feel another person's pain and already your energy field of frequencies becomes weaker. You hear of a tragedy and your field of energy weakens.

Your voltage of your physical body fluctuates depending on your experiences, thoughts, emotions and belief patterns in your life.

When you feel good, your voltage rises and your health is stronger. When you do not feel good, your voltage drops and your immunity system becomes weaker.

When a virus is in touch with you, when the voltage is low within your body, your defense mechanisms are lower and thus contracting an illness becomes easier at that very time for there is less resistance to fight the illness.

Your immunity system does not only exist on your physical, biological level but also on the higher energetic levels. These higher levels are your first form of defense against any illness.

Imagine for a moment, you have large fields around your physical body. You may not be able to see them with your eyes, but they are there. They are constantly moving and are constantly connecting with each other. Each part is important, and each part helps you to stay strong and balanced when it is in balance.

Imagine you have an electric wired fence all around you. You are perfectly designed and if you could understand the beauty of your creation, you could learn how to release disease and truly heal as a race.

If you could grasp the power you have over your cellular level and how you could plug into greater light, you would find your strength and great wellness as a race.

Again, we go back to the fear and the pain. These create energy imbalances. When there are energy imbalances, there are energy weaknesses. These weaknesses allow illness to form.

Your electric wire grid within and around your energy body of light carries a high charge.

When viruses, which also are highly energetic, approach this defense mechanism, it protects you energetically. The virus cannot affect your field as much.

However, when your defense mechanism within the field of light is lower, the virus can then breed and cause damage and make you feel very ill.

Fear, distress, anger, loss and self-denial cause imbalance within your energy defense mechanisms.

These are your greatest weaknesses. In order to bring back the balance, these weaknesses will have to be released and be replaced with Greater Love.

Fear feeds a virus and the greater the fear is, the greater the virus is able to multiply and thrive in an energetically depleted zone.

When a person carries Great Love from a higher source and carries self-love, the energy field has a protective shield to keep the physical body stronger. The virus will not be able to attack as much, or not at all.

Imagine for a moment, you are building this defense mechanism around yourself. You are building a grid of light to protect your body from disease and imbalance. Imagine you are building your inner strength to help you become stronger.

A Komo Ha Halima, Greetings and Love from the Pleiadian Realms of Light, I AM AMMORAH, Pleiadian High Priestess, assisting you to greater health and love.

A Komo Ha Halima

Greetings, I AM AMMORAH

Pleiadian High Priestess on the Pleiadian High Council

Part 58: Working with your energy grid

Imagine, you have a grid around you. You are able to learn to define strong boundaries around this grid and receive the life you desire, or you can choose to walk in ignorance, never understanding about the most incredible part of your learning – your Sacred Energy Field.

Each energy field is connected to greater energy fields. Each has dimensions within itself, waiting to be discovered and 'remembered' by the owner, which is you.

When you awaken, you begin to realize the magnificent being you are. You are gifted with depth beyond your imagination at this very moment. All will be realized when it is time.

In this moment of time, you are learning to work with many areas in the Sacred Energy Body. You are discovering energy within your energy field is able to be replenished or it can greatly weaken as areas can 'seep' energy out.

Pain and fear are the main causes for energy depletion. When you fear something, you are focusing upon it and it will be created within your life because you set the rules and laws in your universal system to play out the dance.

Please understand your energy is constantly in motion, creating your life based on your beliefs, desires, views, fears, anger, pain, regrets, hope, love, lack of love, attitudes and thought patterns.

Energy leaves your energy field when you do not feel great inner strength. It is then that you 'allow' your energy to leave your energy 'grid' to go to others who are claiming it as their own.

When you lack strong self-identification, it is regarded as an energy disease because your energies will become greatly depleted, which causes great unbalance.

To learn to build a strong energy field to have a wonderful life, strong health and a life where you will learn to create your success and your dreams, you must learn to have great self-love and to build a strong relationship with yourself.

You must learn to own who you are and be proud of yourself. You must learn to identify strongly with yourself.

When you make decisions, it is not based on other people's ideas or views but it is because it comes from your truth.

Here again, the lesson is to find your greater inner truth. When you are persuaded by other people to take another direction and you believe in other people's opinions and ideas, your own energy field becomes greatly depleted.

You are freely giving your energies away to the ones who have strong opinions, to the ones you listen to.

Your game is to find truth in this. You will find it by discovering your deeper connection within yourself.

You must observe when you feel strong and when you feel depleted. You must learn to understand the moment your strength is leaving.

Everything is an energy play. Energy constantly moves. It never stops moving and it never stops creating.

When you desire to build a grid around you that is strong, you must create boundaries for yourself first. You must understand what your rules are of your own universal system.

What will you do in your life and what will you not do in your life? What do you believe in? Do you believe you are strong enough to carry out your higher purpose, or do you feel limited?

We are asking you to pull yourself into the present moment. In the present moment your energies are much stronger as they are contained within the grid, thus you have greater 'electrical power.' Your charge is higher.

When you are in fear and pain and when you carry anger, you are not in the present moment. Your energies are greatly fractured and scattered. They are not focused upon healing and your confusion and anger becomes greater.

Focus upon your energies and pull them back to you. Claim them back to you and be with them. Command them to come back to you in the highest way and then clear them. By commanding them to be cleared, your energies will be able to create greater change and areas of greater growth in your life.

When you claim them back you are building your energy grid of light.

When you build an energy grid you also build your own inner power and you are securing your energy grid.

When you secure your energy (or anchoring), you become more within your purpose. You become stronger and you become more in the flow of who you truly are.

When you have an insecure self, your life will reflect this back to you. You begin to depend too much on others or on situations within your life, such as your work. You forget to look within. You forget to anchor deep within and feel the strength and love from within.

This is why many people who do not feel secure become greatly unbalanced within their lives and they become lost as they cannot move forward with truth and strength.

Many people feel empty, disconnected, unsatisfied and lonely. The love for life is not there. They do not understand their greater reasons for life. For them it is difficult to journey within their hearts and to feel their heart. They are out of touch with their emotional self, constantly looking for purpose and reason.

It is similar to floating in the ocean, forever looking for land but not finding it. It is as if forever searching for an anchor to moor, but floating further into the distance without a map and without guidance.

These are the hollow spaces of emptiness.

On the way to searching for an anchor to have fulfillment and love, many often become controlling, seeking to find security in others, seeking to find the missing pieces that only can be truly found when they have the courage to journey within.

To become secure within self requires a new focus. It requires higher awareness and courage to look at life in a new way, as if new glasses were given to see another perspective of life.

A Komo Ha Halima, I AM AMMORAH, Pleiadian High Priestess, helping you to understand your great inner beauty.

Spiritual Strengthening
Building the flows of love

Exercise 19: Learn to bring balance and love in your life

1. For a moment, relax and bring in the Great Light. Breathe the light into your bodies. With every breath in you feel the light expanding within you.

2. Call in the High Beings in the Universe. Call us also, as your Pleiadian healers.

3. We ask you to become calm and to feel connected to your earth. Connect to your feet and connect deeply to your planet.

4. Share your love with your planet.

5. Say with a firm voice, 'I command my energies to be with me, healed in the Great Light to create strength, love, wisdom and abundance in my life.

6. 'To all my weaker energies that no longer serve me and do not belong to me any longer, I say, GO NOW! Become healed in the light.'

7. Bring your focus within and feel connected. Release yourself with the breath.

8. Well done with this powerful exercise of building strength.

Spiritual Strengthening
Building the flows of love
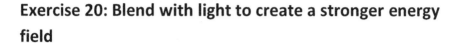

Exercise 20: Blend with light to create a stronger energy field

1. Breathe in and out slowly and relax your body.

2. For a moment let all your daily activities go and focus on your breath in and out.

3. Surround yourself with light by asking for it and breathe in light and breathe out light.

4. Imagine a light above you. This light desires to blend with you to help you become stronger and to help you appreciate who you are. It helps you understand you are loved by the light.

5. Visualize a magnificent sun above you. Feel this light coming inside of your crown. It moves down slowly and gently.

6. Feel the light blending deep within your heart now. You are now feeling more greatly loved and feeling appreciated by the light.

7. Imagine you are letting go of all your anxieties now. Do not worry about anything or anyone at this time and simply be in the moment. Feel strong and anchored deep within you. With each moment, feel greater strength building as you are sitting in this light.

8. Afterwards, slowly breathe in and out and come back fully to your plane.

The love Angels have for you

You are loved by Angels,

who support your growth.

Learn to set yourselves free,

in the light.

Learn to celebrate,

your magnificence,

your internal power,

your great gifts.

Draw in love.

Learn to shine.

Learn to be.

LOVE!

A Komo Ha Halima

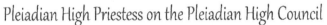

Greetings, I AM AMMORAH

Pleiadian High Priestess on the Pleiadian High Council

Part 59: Your thoughts create your experiences

Your thoughts are incredibly important. Constantly your thoughts and energy are in motion to create your life.

You are the law maker for your own life and your thoughts and energy create your life depending on how you have formed your belief systems.

You are also able to take on belief systems of other people and the world and create experiences based on their belief systems.

Again, here are lessons of learning to be truthful to self and learning to be forgiving. Do not hold on to the pain of others and do not allow your energies to be depleted.

You must learn to claim who you are and love who you are.

Constantly you direct energy with your focus. The greater your focus is on your thoughts and emotions, the stronger the energy play becomes.

All is a lesson and an experience. You are here to learn to control your thoughts and your energy play. You are here to learn to master your world collectively and individually.

Once you begin to understand these lessons, you will be able to focus upon the healing for your own lives and for your world.

Imagine you are a central station with many types of vehicles. Some of these vehicles are slower than others.

With your focus, with your thought, with your heart, you are producing the engine power for these vehicles.

At times you may select certain vehicles to go faster and you achieve this by concentrating on these particular vehicles greater.

Some of the vehicles move towards a wonderful holiday destination. You as the driver see the vision and desire to have a holiday with peace and love.

Because you are in the high flows of love constantly, leaving all pain behind, great things happen. This is because you are in the flow of creation.

Your life moves faster, and greater events and experiences are yours to have.

Some vehicles have difficulty starting. They complain and sputter. They feel drained and need lots of work doing to them. They do not achieve the great result because they are not in the flow of creation and love.

Thus, the lesson here is, understand where your energy is flowing towards. Is it focused on love and success, or on frustration in life?

Here is the choice. You are learning to understand you are the master of your own lives.

Every thought you create depends on where your vehicles travel to and at what speed.

The more you focus upon your thoughts, the greater your play becomes. Each has a destination, lessons and experiences.

You continuously send out signals. Your energy body is constantly creating your life.

If you understood the power within you, you would quickly learn to focus upon love and greatness. You would awaken to the play upon your earth.

By holding on to pain energies, you are creating the same over again. This is because you focus upon it. Where your focus is, your energy follows. The rules of the Cosmic Dance are always the same.

When your fear is intense, you are creating your fears to become your reality. They hold a tremendous amount of strong frequencies.

Imagine sending out signals constantly to your fears. Your fears then become part of your dance play because you always invite your fears to your Cosmic Dance.

By focusing upon your fears, you allow them to become a friend to you. You give them the invitation and they will not refuse, unless you begin to shield yourself from your fears and allow them to be cleared.

When you are angry, your focus is also tremendous.

The more you build your anger, the weaker your energy field becomes and thus you become more open to greater pain coming in your life for you to experience.

You will keep dancing this way until you begin to learn to change your ways of being and your ways of doing.

Your focus upon your desires is crucial in this game of life. What do you focus your attention on?

In this plane you are on, you are learning to understand the game. The greatest game on your plane is to learn to stand away from your fears and your pains and focus on your greatness and your desires, knowing everything is an illusion and you are here to become free from pain to stand in your creator power.

When you claim who you are, when you love and appreciate who you are and stand in the truth of who you truly are, when you focus your thoughts on wonderful desires, with a heart filled with love and great inner passion, you are creating wonderful things in your life.

A Komo Ha, Halima, I AM AMMORAH. I desire to help all people who desire love upon your plane to rise to the higher cosmic dances. The gate is now open for all who choose to learn to dance higher. The healings from Divine Love are now happening upon your plane for all who choose to rise in the love and who choose to dance to the higher beat of love.

A Komo Ha Halima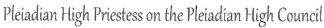

Greetings, I AM AMMORAH

Pleiadian High Priestess on the Pleiadian High Council

Part 60: Every thought creates power

The thought itself does not carry any energy at all. Its charge is nil. However, when the thought is created with an intention, this sparks a charge. The greater the pain or the love of the intention, the greater the charge of that frequency becomes.

Each thought, accompanied by an intention creates power, depending on the focus and the emotion attached to the thought.

You create energies constantly. When you create energies, you send them out. Your energy bodies desire to carry out your command as you are the commander of your personal universe.

As you can see, when groups of people send out similar energies, this play intensifies.

When you are unaware of the great power you have, you can create much pain together.

All is an illusion. All is a game. Learn to play the game wisely.

A positive charge is far greater than a negative charge.

However, if the thought frequency holds both positive and negative charges, there could be a play of both charges playing out their frequencies of pain and joy simultaneously, each playing their own dance.

When you play in the cosmic parties, learn to become more conscious of where you direct your focus towards.

You will become more observant as to what energy does and how it works.

You are marvelously connected and created. It is not until you begin to understand the energy game and the game of life that you begin to comprehend the beauty of your life.

When you fully participate in life and understand the importance of your emotions, your life becomes a joy and hence your life will reflect more joy and happiness.

You constantly create and the more consciously you play the game, the greater you will yearn to learn how to create higher plays of energies.

Love is the greatest universal force in all of creation. Love creates all. Love understands all. Love fills life with glory.

You are the creators of your Dance of Light. You create your life constantly and depending on the energies you choose to dance with, depends on your Dance of Play.

We, as Pleiadians in the light, dance with the light. We focus upon our light. We understand the greatness of the Light Dance and the Cosmic Dance we are playing with as Star Love Beings.

You are invited to the Great Party of Light and to play at the Great Light Party. We encourage you to learn to focus upon your thoughts as your thoughts will constantly create your experiences in life.

All is an illusion. All is a choice. Choose for the greater choices.

A Komo Ha Halima, peace be with you. Greetings, from AMMORAH, Pleiadian High Priestess, assisting you with your journey to Greater Light.

Spiritual Strengthening
Building the flows of love

Exercise 21: Strengthen your flow

1. Allow yourself to relax by breathing in and out deeply. Call in the light of the Angels and also call in your Pleiadian healers of light.

2. After a few moments of relaxing begin to feel within your body. Where is it you are feeling the tension? Is it in your heart? Is it in your hips? Is it in your throat? Is it in your neck? Begin to sense deeper.

3. As you sense your body, breathe in light and send it to the area where tension is held. Allow yourself to feel once again and feel how relaxed you are.

4. Allow yourself to say the following words: 'Fear is no longer a part of me. I allow it no longer to be a part of my life. I no longer hold myself a hostage to my fear.

5. 'I allow myself to be in the light now. The light will guide me to love and peace. The light will give me my strength. I will remain focused upon the light. The light will free me.

6. 'I forgive all that has hurt me and caused me pain and fear. I allow myself to rest in the light of the Angels.'

7. Slowly allow yourself to come back with the breath.

A Komo Ha Halima

Greetings, I AM AMMORAH

Pleiadian High Priestess on the Pleiadian High Council

Part 61: Choosing your flow of existence

This great Dance Party of Light is asking you one of the most important questions in all cosmic plays. Which illusion will you learn to dance with? You can create different illusions for your learning and each flow depends on your play of your thought-power and your focus.

When you play in pain illusions you will have trouble flowing with higher light because your thoughts do not flow in light.

When you flow with pain you will have difficulty grasping these lessons unless you are opening your mind and your higher heart to appreciate and desire to understand these lessons.

You always have the choice to learn to create higher experiences in life with great focus, determination and great love.

You live in parallel existences together. You create different energy flows together. You create different outcomes of your flows of existence together, depending on how flows are created by you.

If you desire to live in a certain flow of life, you have the choice to learn to create this. You can learn to become 'anchored' into the existence you choose to have.

When you choose to live in a higher 'reality,' your thought flow and your focus will move towards the higher 'reality.' Thus, you begin to align yourself with higher flow.

As you already have learned much about the choices you have, we ask you to celebrate with your universe. You have a choice of freedom. You can choose not to align with higher frequencies and stay in the anger, fear and pain, or you can choose to work towards the love frequencies and the higher power frequencies of love alignment.

We are not saying this choice will be easy for you, for any energy movement at any stage requires to be pushed through with love and determination. There will always be a push and a pull moving towards a high level.

For many thousands of years, the fall of consciousness brought you into spiritual darkness. This meant humanity lost their greater choices of aligning to light dimensions. You were thrown about like waves of the ocean.

You forgot about the greater energies at play. You forgot why you were created. You believed stories and these stories carried a thought-power frequency. Thus, you began to anchor yourselves within these stories and these became your 'truth.' You began to be anchored into your 'truth' together. You began to believe in the illusion together.

Because you needed to be anchored into an energy of flow to exist in, you decided as a race to be influenced greatly by these stories and thus you gave these stories a greater charge. All charges give and pull freely.

When you believe in other people's stories and create it as your own truth you freely give your energy to others because you believe in their truth. This is how these stories of 'truth' will gain stronger power flow to create stronger stories of pain upon your plane.

We understand these teachings may seem new to you. Because your existence is entirely free-will, you freely can give your power away to anyone who has the greatest evidential story of 'truth.'

You are free to investigate how your world plays out its 'reality,' based on stories that were created to help you forget your true history.

You talk about parallel existences in universes, but do you not understand these parallel existences also play out on your earth?

You have parallel choices and choices of walkways to choose from. Which walkway of existence will you choose? Which game will you look at? Which will you choose for yourself?

You can explore many ways of existence, depending on your choices.

Fear and pain keeps you in your limitation, whereas joy and love helps you to expand.

If we told you, you were able to choose a higher flow of existence and learn to live it, would you desire this higher existence? Or would this concept be too difficult to comprehend?

Many of you are ready to begin to learn and understand the choice of living in higher walkways of energy play could well be possible.

Many, because it is too difficult to comprehend these higher levels, like to stay limited in their own existence of their living 'reality' and do not truly desire change. They desire peace on your plane but are not willing to take part in the freedom change.

They are not willing to change their ways of thinking because they do not understand higher 'realities.'

They define life with denser 'realities' and thus for them to change to a higher 'reality,' a great shift within their consciousness needs to happen before they can allow higher thinking to take place. They are freely giving their power to the existence of pain and fear flows.

It is not until many of you find this higher existence together and create definite change on your plane together, that those who freely give their power to the existence of pain and fear will surrender to the Higher Play of Life.

This play is ultimately your choice. It is your choice to dance in the Great Light or to dance the Pain Dance. After all, you are the creators of your plane.

Awaken within to find your freedom.

A Komo Ha Halima, I, AMMORAH, am asking many people upon your plane if they are ready to dance in the higher cosmic spaces. If you say yes, please begin to act upon it and learn to dance to the frequencies of the higher star dimensions. The Great Healings are taking place at this time to allow you to become free in your dance. Will you desire it enough to act upon it?

A Komo Ha Halima

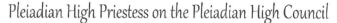

Greetings, I AM AMMORAH

Pleiadian High Priestess on the Pleiadian High Council

Part 62: Learning to find your higher dance of light

You have already discovered the strength and love throughout these pages. We have visited many areas of how you can learn to create greatness together.

You may like to use this book as a life manual, to live by for a while until you understand the lessons and then you will celebrate learning higher lessons still.

Each one of you has greatness within and it is when your teacher within you awakens that is when you are ready to dance higher with greater alignment.

Your inner teacher, when it awakens, is keen to help you find your Higher Dance of Light to greatly empower you. The Dance of Light carries a high charge to help you flow with a greater life.

When you find your Teacher within you will be blessed, and you will dance with the Great Cosmic Energies of Light and then you will be ready to be carried up higher.

There is no end to learning how to dance higher. When you learn how to dance higher, your happiness, inner peace and great joy of life becomes greater because your energies of play become higher.

This is because the Teacher of Light within you carries a great charge. This higher charge raises your voltage and thus your health and abilities on all levels of your existence becomes greater.

You then begin to understand you are not limited but you carry the charge of your own creator power within you.

This is the power you have been looking for, for many lifetimes.

Learning to find it can be challenging for you because this requires looking within your deepest self. When you have always given your power away to the stories you have believed in, you have great difficulty looking within for the answers.

These are the great power battles of energy games in your existence.

You are now learning to claim your power back.

Here, we as Pleiadians in the Light say, learn to focus on your own power. How do you desire to live your flows of life? Do you desire to change your dance of life?

How much have you given your powers away to the stories to create flows of pain and anger? How much have you become entangled within this maze of painful illusions?

To become entangled is relatively easy to do. All you need to do to become entangled is to be close to someone who upsets you with their anger. You believe it is your anger and you become angry and in pain.

You may listen to a certain event on your television screens and you become drawn into the show of that particular 'reality' and you make it your 'reality.'

Which flow do you choose to live in? Where do you choose to tune into?

You have different frequencies on your plane. You are like a radio station, constantly sending out transmissions and receiving transmissions. You are able to read them well and translate them to create a greater picture. This will depend also on the voltage of your personal play as to how flows affect your life.

If you carry a lower voltage, then it is easier for you to listen to the lower frequencies of play. You attract these lower frequencies into your play because you attract them into your dance.

When you learn to listen to higher love frequencies, you begin to open to higher choices. You desire change upon your plane and you choose not to listen to pain, anger and fear. You choose to stay clear from the pain and to free yourself from fear to keep playing higher.

Your desire to find the great teacher within you becomes greater once you align higher. Therefore, your 'reality' of life will change phenomenally.

Once more the different ways of dance is your free choice. Which 'reality' will you choose? Will you choose to dance with pain, fear or anger, or will you choose to dance with love?

When you are ready to listen, you will find your teacher. It will only be discovered by those who desire to dance with the Light Dance Party, as then you become awakened to all truth and to the greater 'realities.'

When your teacher shows up, you (the student) are ready to listen. It will guide you to your greatness and all your questions will be answered. This dance becomes easier to live. It becomes higher with plays of love. The choices of the dance become greater as the student is taught how to play higher and how to create greater.

Therefore, if you are willing to open to this we can give you a transmission right now to allow you to find your teacher within you, to be in that light and to feel the light.

Anyone and everyone can join in this light. You are from the light. It is your choice however to find the light once again within your heart.

A Komo Ha Halima, we are your Pleiadian Healers of Great Love, assisting mankind back to a journey of light and to find the wisdom within you.

Spiritual Strengthening
Building the flows of love

Exercise 22: Call your teacher

1. Breathe in the light and breathe out the light. Feel relaxed and allow your body to relax.

2. Surround yourself with your Angels and state clearly your intention to find the teacher within you, to allow you to discover greater guidance and greater flows of life.

3. Breathe in light deeper and breathe out light deeper.

4. Visualize and feel your lungs becoming light and your sacred eye becoming light.

5. Visualize and feel your spiritual heart becoming light and feel it expanding as great as possible in the light.

6. Imagine for a moment a Teacher of Light stands in front of you. You may see this Teacher in your inner mind as you open to these higher flows of light.

7. Ask the Teacher to join you and to assist you to your higher path.

8. Feel your heart filled with so much love for your Teacher as your Teacher has so much love for you.

9. Stay in that play of energy until you have finished.

10. Upon finishing, come back again, fully present and grateful.

A Komo Ha Halima

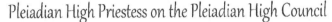

Greetings, I AM AMMORAH

Pleiadian High Priestess on the Pleiadian High Council

Part 63: The illusion of energy play

Learning to play higher in the light means to change patterns of your previous ways of play. You now desire to understand how to create greater success in your life and to awaken the creator within you.

Imagine the greatness you could create. Which door would you choose to open? Which 'reality' would you choose to live? After all, your life and your existence upon your plane is all an illusion of energy play.

Please understand this. Your life is an illusion of energy play. It is not solid. It is not fixed.

Illusions can change depending on your focus and on your game of existence.

When you choose to focus on higher flows of existence, you carry a higher charge and therefore you will create a higher existence. When you believe your life to be 'fixed' and to be an absolute 'reality,' your life will be limited because after all, your life is an illusion.

When you live your life as 'fixed' and 'real,' you will play that particular game, for all your beliefs become your play.

Many people on your plane believe in 'fixed reality' because they are suffering. They are far from happy and do not play in the higher dimensions upon your plane but fully participate in the lower dimensions of pain.

Many who live in these painful energies are old souls who came to your plane as brave beings desiring to awaken you, to show you, you are the ones who need to change before you can bring about the great change.

This is why many are playing the game of war and poverty. The task to bring peace and love to your plane is great for you as light workers. Are you willing to participate in the change? Or will these ones continue to suffer until you decide you are ready to change your beliefs systems? All play the game of life to awaken each other upon your plane.

Before you recognized the higher plays of how to bring change to your existence, you may have played your games differently. You may have felt there were no other options other than rebelling, fighting or protesting.

However, do you not see the energy game at play? Do you not see when you do these very things you are giving your power and energy away to the very things you detest? These energies of pain only become stronger and thus their play of strength becomes stronger.

It would be better for you to learn how to bring change in higher ways once you understand what energy does.

When you are angry you are giving the very thing you focus upon a greater energy charge. Therefore, your personal pool of energy decreases and you have less power to dance with higher existence of love.

It is not until you learn to strengthen your energy by plugging into the light to increase your voltage that you will be able to bring about meaningful change.

You came to your plane together to create certain change upon your plane. You knew, in order to bring about change, you needed to come together with one thought and your desires needed to be focused for those changes to come about.

When your desire is strong within your heart of love and your firepower is strong, your charge towards the very things you desire to alter in its frequency within its energy play of existence will change.

Thus, by coming together and creating a strong focus on great visions, you are taking the energy charge away from the things that are painful upon your plane and the energy game will fall in your favor because you play with light.

A Komo Ha Halima, greetings, I AM AMMORAH. I am here with you to guide you towards a greater love, and to help you understand you are the ones who need to change. Learn the ways of love and learn to love all things in your life.

A Komo Ha Halima

Greetings, I AM AMMORAH

Pleiadian High Priestess on the Pleiadian High Council

Part 64: How you play the game of illusion together

It is not until you begin to understand the dance of energy that your plane will change.

You have always succumbed to the fear and anger because this is what your leaders desired you to believe to keep you in your weakness. They took your strength away because you believed their stories.

Now it is essential in your time of existence to understand how to work together in harmony to create change for your plane.

Each day your game of life intensifies.

This is why, when the consciousness of the masses is low, you step into a greater fear dance together.

Greater fear then becomes your 'reality' because you create it together. Greater diseases break out when your voltage is lower. Your financial markets do not do well when you come into fear together. Masses receive pain in certain areas because of the fears you have created together.

You are the creators of your own pain and fear. We ask you to awaken to the play of energy and to create greater change towards unification and harmony, instead of concentrating on war and anger.

Each day your outcome depends upon your energy play. You celebrate your war veterans and therefore you create more war upon your plane. You teach and discover pain from past world wars and thus you create more energy to discover war with.

You starve yourselves to raise money for the children who starve, which may seem honorable to you, but on the way to saving children you create more hunger upon your plane because you are supporting the energy of poverty. Thus, more people in the future will starve on your plane.

Your protesting to save wild life may seem honorable but you are adding to the pain and this creates more pain and more loss.

Therefore, do you see how you have created much of your own pain upon your plane?

You fight in wars to serve your country because you believe you fight for freedom. What freedom are you fighting for? You certainly are not doing anything to stop your wars and killings. Pain only intensifies.

You desire to stop fish dying in your seas. You make laws to stop needless killing but what you are really doing is creating greater pollution in your seas with your thoughts and more fish are dying than ever before, even without all your fishing.

Your toxic thoughts create greater pollution upon your plane. You fear toxins in your food and you fight against them, but in your fight your body weakens and opens itself to disease caused by toxins because of your very fear.

You fear cancer and thus you talk about it and open yourself to it because of your fear. It would be better for you to meditate and be in the light to learn to clear your fear, to relax in your life and to create greater experiences in your life.

Your anger creates greater anger and spreads like a virus. People feed of these anger energies to create more pain on your earth.

Your fears of sickness are colossal as a race. Hence your immunity system cannot defend itself. You do not understand the beauty of your immunity system resources within your energy body of light.

When your energy body of light is strong you have a force field around you that is electric to prevent the physical layer from becoming sick. However, when there is fear of a particular disease or a bug, the fear creates an opening within the force field which lowers its defenses.

It would be better for you to stay meditating in the light and to clear all your fears from all diseases and visualize a strong light force around your body to keep your electrical gates high to keep your immunity system strong.

You fear terrorism and yet you celebrate it by presenting it on your television screens. You are feeding the energy of terrorism like you have never done before in your history and you create a spectacle each time terrorism occurs. You are feeding the fear and the fear becomes your 'reality' of existence to reflect back to you your belief systems.

You do not understand you create your own pain. Your fears become your 'reality' because of your thought-power play.

In order to change your very 'reality,' you need to change your ways. Each day learn how to change and change in small doses. These small doses teach you to deal in small increments at a time. Your voltage rises and your defense system rises. Greater health will be your outcome.

Your gifts are greater than you can possibly imagine. You are able to create water without toxins, even when water is toxic, by learning to clear it with your innate healing abilities.

You are able to create great nourishing foods of minerals and vitamins for your strength by using your innate healing abilities. You are able to do all this, even when others eat the same toxic food without understanding the concept of clearing.

It is all in the power of your thought play because all is an illusion. Which illusion dance will you play in?

Your physical body is much grander than you could possibly know at this time. It can put up with anything as long as you understand the power of your energy grid within your energy light body.

Your energy light body is strong and more powerful than you can comprehend at this time and it is able to withstand disease and hazards.

When you begin to realize the importance of your energy layers, it is then your medical profession will change. It is then you will begin to understand the beauty of your physical body in greater depth. You will then begin to focus on the greater body, which is the body of light.

This body of light is what you use to awaken your inner creator with. It does not exist in the physical layers but in the energy layers.

Depending on its voltage charge within your energy layers, will depend on how you create your 'realities' of your existences together.

This is what you are required to learn to use in the Great Cosmic Dance of Light. Learn to dance it well and your wishes will come to you.

It will be as if gates open to higher dimensions of play.

A Komo Ha Halima, we are your Healers and Teachers of Light, assisting you to understand greatness within you.

Each moment you create

Each moment in life is precious.

In each moment you create your life.

In each moment you make your choices,

with your focus,

with your vision,

with your thoughts,

with your love,

with your forgiveness.

All of life is an illusion.

It changes in each moment.

Appreciate each moment,

for the next moment,

has already begun.

Spiritual Strengthening
Building the flows of love

Exercise 23: Strengthen your energy body

1. Relax, breathing deeply in and deeply out.

2. Begin to sense within your body. Where can you relax more? Can you bring in love within your body?

3. Forgive all your pain.

4. Call in the light and your Pleiadian healers to surround you with Divine Love.

5. Imagine you are breathing in light and you feel calm. Your lungs become light and you are becoming lighter.

6. Your energy body loves you so much. You have many levels of energy and when you focus on one part becoming stronger, other parts will also become stronger.

7. A large cocoon of light surrounds you. This cocoon is intelligent and knows how you flow in your 'reality' of existence. It desires to help you understand your greater gifts.

8. Imagine a great light connected to your solar plexus. When you breathe in this light, you will feel your solar plexus expanding. Breathe in and out slowly, feeling yourself expanding with every breath.

9. Focus on your heart. Imagine your heart becoming lighter and greater with every breath in and out.

10. Focus upon your sacred eye center. Feel this area expanding into greater light with every breath in and out.

11. Slowly breathing in this incredible energy of light and breathing it out.

12. Relax and be truly grateful for all your healing happening.

Well done.

A Komo Ha Halima

Greetings, I AM AMMORAH

Pleiadian High Priestess on the Pleiadian High Council

Part 65: Working with light in the times of the Great Awakening

Before you can learn to dance in the light that is uniquely yours and to dance with the Great Ones in the Cosmic Dance of Light, it is vital you understand the energies of light and how to interact with them to achieve great unity with light.

At this time, you are working in many frequencies upon your plane. You desired most of all, before you came to the earth at this time of the Great Consciousness of Awakening, to learn to transform the energies of fear and anger to bring it to a greater state of peace and love.

Many of you have worked as light workers in past lives and vowed among yourselves, with each other and with the Great Universe, to do this work of Divine Will Alignment together, to anchor in light, to bring all energies not of light into light to be healed.

You do this in your everyday lives when you understand how to work with them. This does not mean you are required to meditate for hours each day in order to fulfill this sacred obligation.

It means you work your beautiful lives upon your plane and use the powers of light to transform your ways of life into beautiful ways of life. It means learning to become masters upon your plane, learning how to use the powers of manifestation and learning greatness.

You are living in pools of energy illusions. You understand this already. You understand that nothing is solid around you and you are part of the light. You are part of your Prime Creator who desired to explore itself in different ways of existence and in different systems of the universe. You are a part of all this.

All your experiences (as well as all the experiences of all beings in existence) are stored in, what can be likened to a large database to be able to be retrieved for learning and sharing purposes.

You are part of a grand database as it were, and this large database is waiting for the next stage.

This stage is the human race awakening to greatness. It is waiting to see if you begin to understand greatness. It is waiting for you to awaken to your greater discovery, to return to the Great Light, to bring unification to your world and to explore deeper love within.

You have incredible gifts and many in the great space of Universal Existence desire the spiritual gifts you have. They are unique to you and we also desire to explore them once you awaken to them, so that you teach us how to awaken our greater gifts.

Let us work together closer to help you understand who you are and once you have reached your greatness, you in turn help us explore greater depth within ourselves.

We are all Family of Light. You are our Family and we are your Family and we are discovering together the greatness of the light.

Together we can explore greater a greater stage of creation coming and we are asking you, do you desire to work with us as your Family of Light? Do you desire to explore and expand into your greater self? The gate is open for you to be able to explore.

You have made it to this time, and now you are able to choose which path you desire to grow with. It is all up to you our dear friends.

A Komo Ha Halima, I AM AMMORAH, Pleiadian High Priestess. We are your Family of Light.

A Komo Ha Halima

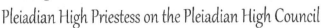

Greetings, I AM AMMORAH

Pleiadian High Priestess on the Pleiadian High Council

Part 66: The element of fear

On your planet you have discovered the fear element well. You have lived it, you have experimented with it and you understand it to be 'real.'

On our planet, our young ones are taught from a young age what energy is. We also teach them what fear is. We give it colors with illustrations and explain how fear travels in waves in a lower frequency.

We teach how energy can be likened to a cloud and how fear travels in clouds of thoughts along with it, waiting for a vulnerable spot within a weak area.

Do you remember the electromagnetic force field we taught you about in previous lessons? When a virus is nearby, and your electromagnetic force field is strong, the virus cannot attack you with great strength. When your electromagnetic force field is weak, the virus can find the weak spots and truly attack you.

Fear, as well as anger, guilt and pain, weaken your force field tremendously and leaves you vulnerable for more attacks by 'fear clouds,' or other people's anger and pain as well as sickness.

Fear clouds are filled with thoughts and beliefs that have not yet become realized. It constantly adds and creates. When a fear cloud becomes strong enough, it will begin to create the thoughts within the cloud to become realized in your 'reality.'

This is what fear does. Like love, fear is also a creation force. However, energies of fear live in lower dimensions. They create great insecurity and pain, far from love.

Fear, like any cloud of energy can grow and take on its own personality as it were and grow with its own desires and thoughts.

For instance, fear can become addictive. Have you noticed in your life how fear can become addictive? You may not realize it but once you fear greatly, to stop fearing is difficult for you.

Why? Because fear is energy that likes to create stability and thus it likes to create more fear to create greater strength.

Many people create clouds of the same fears together and then create its 'reality' to experience their fears together.

For instance, when a group of people concentrate on a certain event or disaster to happen, they are creating it because the cloud of fear carries living, creator force energies.

The cloud of fear also attracts other similar vibrations of fear. It is energy. Energy attracts similar energy fields to create a stable energy field.

You will find when you discover greater love and create greater love, you will attract people with greater love and create higher forms of love in your life that is positive for you to experience and is highly successful.

Fear and anger also seek out energies of the same frequency sound. Each cloud of energy sounds out energy fields that like to grow and expand with other sounds similar to its own frequency zone.

Hence, people's fears become greater and anger becomes greater also. This is the way energy moves. It does what it does, and it is what it is. Energy frequencies create stronger energy frequencies. Energy never stops expanding.

When you have strong willpower, you can transform the energy cloud of fear into a higher energy cloud of love. Transmutation creates a harmless field of energy so that it can be converted to love and power.

You are able to neutralize your fears and then move them into the power zone of success and love. This is your ability when you know how to do this.

However, to work with transmutation, it is important to understand how energy moves and creates. You have the ability to neutralize it and transform the lower energies into higher forms. Your thought-power and firepower are incredibly effective regarding transmutation and transformation.

Constantly your energy moves and seeks to expand. You control energy with your thought-power. You are able to dance with it or lose control with it.

Fear energy is addictive and carries a form of intelligence. It knows when it is about to be changed. It is not easy to dance with as it will give you thoughts of, 'It is not real. It is not going to change.'

Your battles will be great. This is why it is important to have a strong mind with strong thought-power and willpower to change your energy play.

Once you awaken to the energy play, your game becomes greater and more powerful, as you consciously can make the next moves to create greater play.

Fear can be placed within you from when you were little, from past-life experiences and from beliefs of others. You may have never experienced a certain event before becoming fearful of it, but because fear is an energy to make it seem 'real,' it becomes 'real' and it creates a 'real' situation in your life (depending on how great the energy focus is within the fear), to become your experience.

Your thought process constantly communicates with your energies that you carry. It allows, approves and shuts down constantly. It grows, it shrinks, it allows continuously.

We are going to teach you how to neutralize fear so that your fear does not need to play a part in your 'reality' game. However, will you work with these exercises? Will you allow these exercises to become a part of your daily life?

A Komo Ha Halima, I AM AMMORAH, Pleiadian High Priestess. We are here to guide you to a life filled with love, without fear.

Spiritual Strengthening
Building the flows of love

Exercise 24: Transmute your fear

1. Relax your body, breathing in and breathing out slowly. Always call in the Great Light of the Angels for healing and for balancing. Call in your Pleiadian healers also.

2. Begin to tune into your own energy.

3. Begin to focus upon the fear energy that you carry.

4. Your fear energy has a color. What color does it have? What do you see or perceive?

5. We invite you to talk to your fears. 'Fear, from this moment, you hold no power over me any longer. I clear you now in the name of the Divine Light.'

6. Then you forgive it with saying: 'I forgive, release and let you go in order for my healing to happen. So be it.'

7. You are now freer to play with your higher energies of love.

8. Slowly breathe in and out and come back.

Well done.

A Komo Ha Halima

Greetings, I AM AMMORAH

Pleiadian High Priestess on the Pleiadian High Council

Part 67: Playing life awakened

Your inner spirit will grow with great strength when it is loved by you. You must learn and accept your spirit is a part of who you are. You are part of your spirit and your spirit is a part of you.

When your spirit is a part of you with your love, you begin to truly love who you are. To recognize your spirit nurtures you deeply.

As you have already learned much about your spirit, it is now you are ready for this next lesson.

When you fill yourself with more of your spirit, your energy field strengthens which supports your greater health and expands your life.

With this stronger field of love, you are able to reflect your greater opportunities and discoveries in your life. You are building a greater foundation of greatness and love.

Like a body builder constantly building up his or her body for competitions, you are also building up your energies for greater love and life experiences.

This training for greater strength takes a small amount of sacrifice. You train to walk in the light and in its greatness. The stronger your energy field is, the stronger your spirit is able to house within you, to allow you to have grander and stronger experiences of life.

Your spirit flows love through your body. It protects your body from harm and it allows your body to move with greater light.

You are able to understand that all is an illusion when it flows strongly within you as it constantly guides you to greatness and love.

When you dance with your spirit, you will constantly seek to please your spirit. You feel drawn to listening to it and it becomes a grander part of you.

Your intuition strengthens, and your spiritual abilities become stronger as you are playing with higher energies of love and light and thus you are building a solid foundation for your growth and higher understanding.

No longer are you walking in separation and misunderstanding. Now you are gaining a higher understanding of your life and your purpose. Your grander purpose is becoming more known to you and you are guided with more strength.

This is the dance between your human self and your spirit self. It is the ultimate dance you can perform in your existence of your dimensional play. When you can dance to this beat, it becomes greater and you embrace it because this is your dance. Your dance is unique and it is personal to you.

Everyone will have their personal dance of spirit and human self. Everyone will experience it differently when they find the dance.

Everyone who finds it will receive the greatest love and the greatest union possible.

It is then, you will discover your magnificence and your love, for all of life is grand. Your flow begins to dance greater and the beat is picking up. You invite others to your dance as your life has changed from being unaware, to now becoming very aware of the relationship and the dance between yourself and your spirit self.

You rejoice and celebrate every moment. You embrace your spirit and your spirit embraces you. Your words become more of love. You embrace everything you do because you love your spirit. You communicate with it. You heal with it. You can build a passionate relationship between yourself and your spirit.

To be able to build a strong relationship between your spirit and you, it is important to be open to it, to meditate often and to invite your spirit to communicate with you.

Thus, you will find a stronger connection with yourself and with your life. You will become filled with joy and strength as you walk your path of life and dance with the love in the light energies.

We, Pleiadian healers in the light desire very much to be a part of your healing and we desire to be your closer friends to guide you to the greater dancing steps in the Dance of Light.

The steps in the cosmic energies of light and love are quick. They are rewarding and loving.

They are enjoyable and the more your spirit joins you, the greater your desire will be to dance with us.

A Komo Ha Halima, I AM AMMORAH, Pleiadian High Priestess. May you find your freedom and live greatly.

A Komo Ha Halima

Greetings, I AM AMMORAH

Pleiadian High Priestess on the Pleiadian High Council

Part 68: Awakening your deeper Universal Codes

We have already discussed throughout these pages much about your focus and your thought-power. At this time, we would like to invite you to reflect on your own journey in life.

We are your friends and your tutors. We desire to teach you greatness to step into the Greater Dance with your Angels of Love.

As you have learned, you hold the codes of your universe within you because you belong to this part of the universe.

We also hold codes within our light bodies of our universal systems and they date back a long, long time, well before your creation. We have not always lived on the Pleiades and thus we also hold the codes from our other universal existences.

These codes hold different keys waiting to be revealed by you, waiting until you learn to dance with them.

The greater your Cosmic Dance becomes, the greater these keys will open for you. They will help you to understand your beauty and your perfection. They will help you to understand you are not small beings but indeed you are strong creators.

You hold gifts from your forefathers, your ancestors and your Creators. Your Creators are magnificent beings. They hold the keys of the Greater Universe and you are a part of this also.

They desired to create you with deep perfection. They had an understanding of what could happen with your DNA that could lead to great pain and disharmony. They knew the probability of great interference with your DNA was incredibly high.

Your Creators have not discovered the pain you have discovered. They have never discovered separation and loss of life like you have. They do not understand pain of death and sickness like you do. They do not understand war and crime like you do. They live in an existence beyond all pain that you know very well.

They are magnificent beings and they knew, in order to explore whether you would learn to dance in light again, you would most probably be tested and discover suffering and pain.

Hence, they placed deep codes within your DNA. These codes would always remain there despite the pain and the suffering you would probably discover together and as individuals.

These codes would only be awakened when you would find your deep spiritual love. You would hear the Universe calling to you when it was time to awaken and then these codes would awaken to deeper spiritual gifts within you.

At this time your Creators are awaiting your results collectively and are closely watching your DNA heal and how you will progress within your lives.

A time will come, when these healings will accelerate beyond your ability to comprehend at this time. This will be a time when you will have passed the test together. The test of, will you remember the light? Will you return to the light within your heart despite the darkness and the pain upon your plane?

When you do, your light will return and your powers will return. This is when your true greatness will return to you.

We eagerly look forward to this time also, for you hold greater gifts within you which we are keen to understand. Then you can help us understand your greatness as we will be able to share with you our greatness.

How wonderful it will be to dance together in these physical dimensions of light, you and us, dancing our Cosmic Dance of the Great Family of Light.

Can you behold this image within your mind? Would you welcome your Family in the Light, your Star Brothers and Sisters, in the time of the Great Healing and Acceleration?

We desire this very much. This is the time we greatly long for. To have true peace and unity restored, not only on your earth, but in the entire Universal Existence.

How wonderful it will be also for your Creators, your Star Fathers and Mothers in the light. Your Prime Creator will also be very happy, because then everything will be in alignment and everything can come back to its ultimate perfection.

It will be a time of celebration, a time of rejoicing, a time of deeper love and deeper union.

At that time, there is no more pain on your planet, no more fear, no more anger, no more illness and no more poverty. All these things will have been done away with.

However, dear ones, what is required from you to get there? Is it going to be a sudden change? Will it be changed overnight?

It will not happen in a short moment. This requires a change of your consciousness and the way you flow in your life.

Much work is ahead of you. You will discover in the next few lessons what is required from the players on earth and the greater purpose.

A Komo Ha Halima, I AM AMMORAH, Pleiadian High Priestess, assisting you to awaken to the Great Light.

A Komo Ha Halima

Greetings, I AM AMMORAH

Pleiadian High Priestess on the Pleiadian High Council

Part 69: Alignment with cosmic flows

The hosts of the Great Cosmic Party invite all who desire to live within the heart.

They promise they are good hosts and they promise many blessings. They promise that all love and enjoyment at the Great Dance Party will be given to all their guests. They are good entertainers and have good food, drink and music.

The alignment within the Cosmic Party is grand. It is not easy to follow all the steps and like any dance, some practice is needed but once everyone aligns, great rewards will be theirs to have.

Not everyone on your planet is required to be aligned to great love in order for change to happen on your planet. If only a small part of your earth's total population would learn how to work with greatness and discover their creator within, it would be enough to bring change to your planet and help more people awaken to light.

Perhaps you look at your world and you see the pain and war. It is not encouraging for you to turn on the television screens and see people protesting, fighting, suffering from anxiety and dying.

This, for you, instills a greater desire to bring change.

It is important to focus on what you desire to have, for this becomes your creation of your life. You must learn to do this first before learning how to open up portals of love together to bring change upon your plane.

You must understand if you focus on pain and calamities upon your plane, you are adding to the pain and fear. Then healing upon your plane will take much greater energy to steer the wheel towards love and peace.

If you decided to play different rules to the majority of the people in your world, your world would change quickly if you played the game of energy together.

As you understand already, your world is like a sea of energy. Energies are everywhere, and nothing is as solid as what you believe it to be.

Depending on how the focus is placed upon these energies, they will weaken or strengthen.

When you are in pain, anger and fear, you become depleted energetically because you are feeding into the very things you constantly focus upon.

For example, if you turn on your television and you watch a crime taking place, you become angry and upset. Your energies then feed these energies of crime and the crime is allowed to accelerate because the energy of pain is becoming greater.

If you hold on to pain and the anger, your creator energies stay small and limited.

If you decided to play the game higher, you would be able to use this wisdom to become greater and to bring greater love and success in your own life.

If you focus every day on the very things you love to do and learn to focus on all things that enhance your life, your life would become greater and more loving and therefore you would attract greater experiences towards you also.

Your focus is incredibly important when it comes to finding and understanding your creator within.

How are your energies? Are they strong? Do you feel your inner firepower? Do you carry love within you? Do you feel the determination to carry out your dreams?

If you do, you are dancing with Cosmic Energies of Light.

You are accelerating and climbing up the ascension ladder. You are learning about energies and how to drive them and how to treat them.

Release all your pain, for these pain energies only attract greater pain.

When you do these few things, your life already becomes greatly enhanced as you are learning to steer your creator energies.

Always stay clear of your fear. When you feel your fear, clear them so they have no longer a hold over you and they can no longer disrupt your life.

Everyday discover your fear and work with it. What is to be released? How can you play higher? How can you sing and dance higher in the cosmic energies of love and light?

Focus upon yourself. Focus on your life and how you would like to live your life.

Remember all is energy and you are playing with energy. Create a beautiful world for yourself. Create a world of love and of peace within you. Create wonder within you. Feel greatness always building.

A Komo Ha Halima, we are here to help you understand how to become strong, with flow. Greetings and warm love, from your Pleiadian Spiritual Family, always working in the Great Light.

Spiritual Strengthening
Building the flows of love

Exercise 25: Bring in greatness each day

1. We invite you to relax and breathe in and out slowly.

2. Surround yourself in the light of your Angels by asking for it. With each breath, focus on the light.

3. Visualize love all around you. You are now breathing in the love and breathing out the love, slowly and easily.

4. State, 'I will bring only greatness in my life. I will focus on my strength and my great love. I will focus on living a wonderful life. I will no longer be affected by others. Others have their choice to live. I have my choice to live and I will live with my greatness and my dreams, always with full integrity.

5. 'I allow my dreams to come in now, to help me to dance with the light of my inner fire, to dance with the light of my thought-power. All my dreams will become stronger each time I do this. Each time I work with this I will feel the power within me growing.'

6. Slowly come back with the slow breath in and out.

A Komo Ha Halima

Greetings, I AM AMMORAH

Pleiadian High Priestess on the Pleiadian High Council

Part 70: Accessing your strength to create the life you desire

On your journey in the light you must always keep letting go of your past and be anchored in the present time.

Now in the moment is where you live. Now is where you learn to let go of all your pain and your fear. You are an incredible being with enormous internal power and you can only access your inner strength to create a wonderful life when you are living in the present time.

In the present moment is where you learn to align your inner personal universal system. You align to your own rules and your laws to play the greatest life you can, only when you live in the present time of your existence.

This is where you gain strength. Your thoughts become more aligned with love and greatness and thus your inner power keeps building.

A mountaineer always looks forwards and upwards, never down.

You also, always look up. Always trust the Universe will look after you when you desire to dance the greater steps in the Cosmic Dance of Light.

You are able to bring all desires into your existence. You are able to find the power within you to live your truth within your heart.

To do this, you must learn to discover who you are and to learn to discover your genuine true self.

You are made of different selves. You have a true personality and personalities which are not of truth. These personalities not of truth may be comfortable to you but they are not your genuine personality.

You are beautiful beings and thus you must learn to look beyond the many personalities you have created, to find your true, genuine self.

Fear is also a personality trait. Fear can stop you from living your greatest self. It can stop you from discovering your greater personality and it can stop you from following your truth in your heart.

Fear is a dense energy. It can become very painful for you to live in this dense energy. Many of your people upon your plane live in these dense energies and they do not know how to escape these dense energies of fear.

How has fear stopped you from becoming your greatest? How did you desire to live and how did your fear stop you from reaching your goals and greatness in your lives?

To discover your true potential, it is important to ask these questions. As you begin to question and reason, you may find a personality that is filled with fear.

This is an illusion, for you do not have a true personality made of fear. These are all part of you because you have become accustomed to these parts. You have got to know them very well. You have placed such great power within these 'selves' that you believe you cannot achieve, and lack strength to carry through with your desires and thus your energy has become greatly diminished on your journey of life.

We desire very much to help you understand you hold the gifts of your Creators and they are magnificent beings. They do not understand fear and thus fear is not part of their play.

You must learn to overcome your fear. You must learn to conquer your fear and understand the power it has over you. You attract your fear towards you and if you believe you will succumb to a fear, you will make it happen as part of your experience.

You must learn to become free from your fears by clearing them out of your energy body and understanding that by doing this, you are creating a greater space for you to learn in and to create greatness in.

You are your own creators, in the greatness and in the pain, depending on how you believe you are dancing the steps in your lives and where you place your focus upon.

Are you willing to focus upon greatness and love? Or will you stay within your pain and your fear?

All is a game of illusion. It is all your choice.

A Komo Ha Halima, I AM AMMORAH, Pleiadian High Priestess, guiding you to higher choices to live greater.

A Komo Ha Halima

Greetings, I AM AMMORAH

Pleiadian High Priestess on the Pleiadian High Council

Part 71: Stepping into your future

The future is not yet there for you to experience but it is constantly being created by you in each and every moment.

We have endeavored to help you explore your inner greatness to help you discover your creator energies.

You are your own creators of your life, individually and together. You co-create together. As a group the greater consciousness of your race and you also create your lives individually.

Collective consciousness is creating together. You, with your powers, create the mood of the people worldwide. You all affect each other with your internal belief systems. The greater the pain is on your planet and the greater the people feed into the pain, the greater the pain of the mass consciousness becomes.

You affect each other constantly. You affect each other with the way you sing in your lives. You sing each day your tunes. Some positive and high, some are lower. The question once again is asked; 'which energy do you desire to dance in?'

When your life is strong and balanced, your greatness will come to you.

If you did this in large groups together, you would keep the mass consciousness in a greater and balanced space of life. You could bring the end of all pain upon your planet if you understood how to work with mass consciousness frequencies.

However, before you can work with large amounts of energies for earth healing, you must first learn to focus upon yourself as an individual.

The word focus here is an important lesson in itself. The word focus holds a tight energy of understanding that all energies must be tight and high before greatness becomes a 'reality.'

More than positive thought is within 'focus,' for focus is a strong energy. The energy of focus is of great strength and great determination.

When a soldier upon your planet is focused, he does more than thinking about a positive outcome. He has a goal in mind and within his mind he keeps seeing the goal already at its full completion. He understands very well when he is affected by fear the war has already been lost. One slight mistake and his life could be lost.

This focus is also your key to your greatness within your life. Your quality and greatness of life depends upon your focus. It depends on how tight your energies are and how much you desire to understand the greatness of the steps in your Greater Dance.

Anything that truly is worth exploring deserves great dedication towards the goal. Many of your people become perfectionists with their careers, with their sports, with their arts because they are fully dedicated to their desires.

Surely this journey of energy play is also worth your dedication to begin to study a whole new angle of your life.

Is not your life more important than a sport, a hobby or even a career? For without a career you still have your life, but without your life you cannot have a career.

Your focus upon your future must be great if you desire to learn how to create greatness within your lives.

Walk into the future. What is it you would like to create? Who is it you would like to meet? What is it you would like to do? Sketch it, write it down and listen to the voice within your heart. Feel the greatness and the love.

As you begin to do this, already you are bringing in the energies of the greatness and the love.

Each day think and focus upon what you would like to do in the future. Begin to take little steps each day towards that greatness, already seeing yourself achieving your greatness and your dreams.

You are your own creator upon your plane. The more you believe this to be true, the more you are claiming your creator within and the greater the gifts become for you.

You are an energy learning to work with energies upon your plane. Learn to move it, transform it and to love it. Feel the truth within these words and begin to practice it.

You are a mighty creation, created with great love and mighty intelligence.

A Komo Ha Halima, I AM AMMORAH, Pleiadian High Priestess. May you walk the higher frequencies and discover greatness within. Great Blessings are with you our Dear Ones.

A Komo Ha Halima

Greetings, I AM AMMORAH

Pleiadian High Priestess on the Pleiadian High Council

Part 72: Working in the great expansion work together

Here we begin our conclusion to our pages. We have travelled far together through history and now we are here with you once again.

We are sad to leave you and yet we are happy you have learned so much through these pages.

We have been healing you and sending transmissions of love to you to help you grasp these awakening processes.

Indeed, these are awakening processes. You are awakening your Greater Self with these exercises and your awareness of who you truly are is expanding.

You are living in a time where you are beginning to understand you are far more than human. You were created with a definite purpose and that was to expand, to become greater love, to find your way back home again to the Cosmic Light Dance.

We invite everyone to this magnificent Party of Light. We will teach you more in the future about your multidimensional selves, to help you understand you are a power within your very being.

You hold secrets of all dimensions and all spaces. You are able to reach deep within to understand the energy patterns you have carried through lifetimes. Here you are able to recognize them and to heal them.

You are living in a time we have looked forward to for many thousands of years. We have looked forward to helping you stand in your greater strength, in your greater identification, in your greater self.

How will you use this information? Will you put it away on the shelf, or will you use it and continuously go back to these lessons for deeper learning?

Within these lessons were deeper lessons. Within these lessons were deeper codes and they can only be found by those who truly desire to understand these deeper codes.

The words you are reading were transmitted through a very special channel. This channel knows the sacred secrets of Divine Purpose within her. Thus, because she understands the planes, the dimensions, the structure of the universe and indeed the structure and the purpose of your existence, we have been able to place codes of deeper learning within these words.

You will go from here and awaken more. You will return to these pages and understand you are the key to all your flows.

Will you gather together in groups and decide to do these sacred lessons together? Will you discuss with others how you feel about these words?

UNICEF. (2015). *Education under fire. How conflict in the Middle East is depriving children of their schooling.* Retrieved from www.unicef.org/education/files/EDUCATION-under-fire-September-2015.pdf

United Nations. (1945). The Charter of the United Nations. Retrieved from treaties.un.org/doc/publication/ctc/uncharter.pdf

United Nations. (1945). The Charter of the United Nations. Entered into force October 24. Retrieved from www.un.org/en/charter-united-nations/

United Nations. (1948). Universal Declaration of Human Rights. Adopted by General Assembly resolution 217 A of 10 December. Retrieved from www.un.org/en/universal-declaration-human-rights/index.html

United Nations. (1965). International Convention on the Elimination of All Forms of Racial Discrimination: Adopted and opened for signature and ratification by General Assembly resolution 2106 (XX) 21 December. Retrieved from www.ohchr.org/EN/ProfessionalInterest/Pages/CERD.aspx

United Nations. (1966a). International Covenant on Civil and Political Rights. Adopted and opened for signature, ratification and accession by General Assembly resolution 2200A (XXI) of 16 December. Retrieved from www.ohchr.org/en/professionalinterest/pages/ccpr.aspx

United Nations (1966b). International Covenant on Economic, Social and Cultural Rights. Adopted and opened for signature, ratification and accession by General Assembly resolution 2200A (XXI) of 16 December. Retrieved from www.ohchr.org/EN/ProfessionalInterest/Pages/CESCR.aspx

United Nations. (1979). Convention on the Elimination of all forms of Discrimination Against Women. Adopted and opened for signature, ratification and accession by General Assembly resolution 34/180 of 18 December. Retrieved from www.ohchr.org/Documents/ProfessionalInterest/cedaw.pdf

United Nations. (1989). Convention on the Rights of the Child. Adopted and opened for signature, ratification and accession by General Assembly resolution 44/25 20 November. Retrieved from www.ohchr.org/en/professionalinterest/pages/crc.aspx

United Nations. (2007). Declaration on the Rights of Indigenous Peoples. Retrieved from www.ohchr.org/EN/Issues/IPeoples/Pages/Declaration.aspx

United Nations. (2011). United Nations Declaration on Human Rights Education and Training. Adopted by the General Assembly, Resolution 66/137, A/RES/66/137, 19 December 2011. Retrieved from www.ohchr.org/EN/Issues/Education/Training/Compilation/Pages/UnitedNationsDeclarationonHumanRightsEducationandTraining%282011%29.aspx

United Nations. (2015). *The Millennium Development Goals report.* New York, NY: United Nations. Retreived from www.un.org/millenniumgoals/2015_MDG_Report/pdf/MDG%202015%20rev%20(July%201).pdf

United Nations Committee on the Rights of the Child. (2006). General comment No. 8: The right of the child to protection from corporal punishment and other cruel or degrading treatment (Articles 1, 28 para.2, and 37, inter alia).

United Nations Development Group/ World Bank. (UNDG/WB). (2003, October). Republic of Iraq: Housing and urban management sector needs assessment report. Retrieved from http://siteresources.worldbank.org/IRFFI/Resources/Joint+Needs+Assessment.pdf

United Nations High Commissioner for Refugees (UNHCR). (2015, July 31). *Syria regional refugee response.* Retrieved from data.unhcr.org/syrianrefugees/country.php?id=103

Sweden: Raoul Wallenberg Institute. Retrieved from www.right-to-education. org/sites/right-to-education.org/files/resource-attachments/Tomasevski_ Primer%203.pdf

Tomaševski, K. (2005). *Girls' education through a human rights lens: What can be done differently, what can be made better.* London, United Kingdom: Overseas Development Institute. Retrieved from www.odi.org.uk/events/docs/529.pdf

Tomlinson, S. (2009). Multicultural education in the United Kingdom. In J. A. Banks (Ed.), *The Routledge international companion to multicultural education* (pp. 121–133). New York, NY: Routledge.

Torney-Purta, J., Lehmann, R., Oswald, H., & Schulz, W. (2001). *Citizenship and education in twenty-eight countries: Civic knowledge and engagement at age fourteen.* Amsterdam, Netherlands: International Association for the Evaluation of Educational Achievement.

Torney-Purta, J., Schwille, J., & Amadeo, J. (1999). *Civic education across countries: Twenty-four national case studies from the IEA civic education project.* Amsterdam, Netherlands: International Association for the Evaluation of Educational Achievement.

Turda, M. (2007). Eugenics and the welfare state: Sterilization policy in Norway, Sweden, Denmark, and Finland [book review]. Eds.: G. Broberg & N. Roll-Hansen. *Bulletin of the History of Medicine, 81*(4), 894–895.

UNESCO (1974, November 19). *Recommendation concerning education for international understanding, co-operation and peace and education relating to human rights and fundamental freedoms.* Paris, France: UNESCO.

UNESCO. (1995). *Declaration and integrated framework of action on education for peace, human rights and democracy: Declaration of the 44th session of the International Conference on Education (Geneva, October 1994).* Paris, France: UNESCO. Retrieved from www.unesco.org/education/nfsunesco/pdf/REV_74_E.PDF

UNESCO. (2000). *The Dakar framework for action. Education for all: meeting our collective commitments.* Adopted by the World Education Forum, Dakar, Senegal, April 26–28. Paris, France: UNESCO. http://www.unesco.at/bildung/basisdokumente/dakar_aktionsplan.pdf

UNESCO. (2003, April). *Situation analysis of education in Iraq 2003.* Paris, France: UNESCO. Retrieved from unesdoc.unesco.org/images/0013/001308/130838e.pdf

UNESCO. (2011, August). *World data on education: Iraq* (7th ed.). Geneva, Switzerland: UNESCO. Retrieved from unesdoc.unesco.org/images/0021/002114/211439e.pdf

UNESCO. (2014). *Global citizenship education: Preparing learners for the challenges of the 21st century.* Paris, France: UNESCO. Retrieved from unesdoc.unesco.org/images/0022/002277/227729E.pdf

UNESCO. (2015). *Education 2030: Towards inclusive and equitable quality education and lifelong learning for all.* (Incheon Declaration). World Education Forum 2015, May 19–22. Incheon, Republic of Korea. Paris, France: UNESCO. Retrieved from en.unesco.org/world-education-forum-2015/incheon-declaration

UN-Habitat. (2001). *IDP Site and Family Survey.* Retrieved from mirror.unhabitat.org/list.asp?typeid=3&catid=203

UNICEF. (1990). World Declaration on the Survival, Protection and Development of Children. Agreed to at the World Sunmmit for Children September 30, New York. Retrieved from www.unicef.org/wsc/declare.htm

UNICEF. (2010). *Girls' education in Iraq: A situational analysis.* Retrieved from www.ungei.org/resources/files/full_report_iraq_2010.pdf